A Time to Speak,
A Time to Act

THE MOVEMENT IN POLITICS

JULIAN BOND

SIMON AND SCHUSTER · NEW YORK

To my parents and my wife

Contents

AUTHOR'S NOTE

What follows here is a series of opinions, predictions, some history and thoughts on where black Americans stand in relation to the political process in the United States.

Much of the content comes from speeches, some from previously published material.

It is all the result of several years' travel and work in the United States.

I am grateful to Hal Gulliver, associate editor of the Atlanta *Constitution,* for his invaluable aid in editing and criticizing.

J. B.

Atlanta, Georgia
February 1972

Introduction:
A Prophet Not Without Honor

W. E. B. DU BOIS correctly predicted that the problem of the twentieth century would be the problem of the color line.

With those words, he summed up the crisis that has primarily occupied men and nations and has become the first order of business for millions of oppressed peoples. Racism, the root of the crisis, is as old as the world itself. Internationally, the world's white minority has consistently exploited the resources of the colored majority of the world's population, and has continued to refuse to share the wealth and power it has gained in this way.

Here in the United States the struggle has been taken to the streets of most cities in the country, both violently and nonviolently. It broke out, for a time, on almost every college campus.

It was one part of the struggle that inspired Cuban cane cutters to overthrow a dictator and Vietnamese peasants to resist, ultimately successfully one hopes, through the bitter years, the attempts of outsiders to dominate their homeland. It is also part of the struggle that inspires Alabama sharecroppers to risk their lives in order to have a chance at controlling their destiny, a chance to vote, to find a decent job, to secure a good education for their children.

Dr. Du Bois believed that scientific and rational study of the problems of race and class would yield rational and logical solutions; civilized men, or educated men, are supposed to solve their problems in a civilized manner. That, at least, is what many of us have believed.

But the problems of the twentieth century are so vast, and the resistance to change has been so great, that many have quite naturally been tempted to seek uncivilized solutions. The problems include the poisoning of the air and water; the rape of the land; the new colonialization of peoples, both here and abroad; the new imperialism practiced by Western democracy; and the continuing struggle of those who have not against those who have.

At the birth of what was to become the colossus called the United States, rational and educated men believed that civilization, stretched to its highest order, had begun. Building on a heritage of revolution, expressing a belief in the equality of most, if not all, men, this new democracy was to be the ultimate elevation of men's relationships, one to the other, and a new beginning of decency between nations.

Civilization, as it was then defined, included imposing limitations on war between nations; encouraging the spread of industrialization; the civilizing of so-called heathen elements, these being Indians and blacks; and the harnessing of nature for the benefit and pleasure of man. It was believed generally that man's better nature would triumph over his base desire to conquer and rule and make war, and that intellect, reason, and logic would share equally with morality in deciding man's fate.

Of course it has not been so. Man still makes war; he still insists that one group subordinate its wishes and desires to another; he still insists on gathering material wealth at the expense of his fellows and his environment.

Men and nations have grown increasingly arrogant, and the classic struggle of the twentieth century continues, ever accelerating. The educated peoples of this world have enslaved the uneducated; the rich have dominated the poor; the white minorities have crushed the nonwhite peoples of the globe.

This revolutionary nation—revolutionary two hundred years ago —has become counterrevolutionary. This country, which has visited death on hundreds of thousands of Indochinese, has also found the arrogance to ignore the centuries of pleading for justice from her own domestic colony, the blacks. While these pleadings are dismissed, the central and final issue of the twentieth century comes to the fore, and violence is done to the notion that men can solve their problems without . . . violence. We need to discover just who is and who isn't violent in America.

Violence is black children going to school for twelve years and receiving six years' worth of education.

Violence is almost thirty million hungry stomachs in the most affluent nation on earth.

Violence is having black men represent a disproportionate share of the inductees and casualties in Vietnam.

Violence is a country where property counts for more than people.

Violence is an economy that believes in socialism for the rich and capitalism for the poor. A welfare reform bill, tame and inadequate though it is, can languish in a congressional committee without action even as Congress hastens to pass a loan guarantee bill for hundreds of millions of dollars to bail out an inefficient and financially ailing aerospace company. Socialism for the rich, capitalism for the poor.

Violence is spending $900 per second to stifle the Vietnamese, but only $77 a year per poor person to feed the hungry at home.

Violence is spending $78 billion to kill and only $12 billion to make whole.

Violence is J. Edgar Hoover listening to your telephone conversation; violence is an Assistant U.S. Attorney General—now a Supreme Court justice—proposing concentration camps for white and black militants.

Violence is six thousand American farmers receiving as much as $25,000 each per year not to farm.

Violence is the Congress of the United States putting cotton, tobacco, rice, and cattle ahead of people.

Violence is Richard Nixon and Spiro Agnew ignoring the demands for peace from millions of Americans.

Yet an antidote to *that* violence exists, an antidote that began with Denmark Vesey and Nat Turner, was given impetus by Du Bois and the Niagara Movement, and was spurred on by Martin Luther King, Jr., plus thousands of nameless fighters for freedom.

However, movements are not built on the helpful motions of a few, but by the determined actions of the mass. The chance at power comes in this country not in seizing a dean, but in seizing a welfare office; from organizing a strike of domestic workers; from beginning the arduous process of transferring strength and power from those who have it to those who do not.

This is not easy work. It is not easy because no one wants to do it. In an era of doing your own thing, no one wants to work with and for those whose thing is simply winning and maintaining the right to live. It means more than just the commitment of summer soldiers, although any soldiers are welcome in an understaffed army. It will require serious and systematic allocations of time and energy and resources.

It will require that rhetoric be turned into action, that schoolbook knowledge be applied to street situations, that theories be turned into practice.

It will require that politics comes to mean people and their problems, and not just elections and candidates.

It will require that we build a movement strong enough to take over in a peaceful and orderly fashion; or to seize control, following the example of those who now exercise control.

That suggests there will be no peace. The oppressed of this land will not let peace prevail until they are given power or until they are destroyed by it.

When the day of judgment comes, we shall each have to add up our marks, and those who sat idly by and did nothing until that day shall be the first to go. But it will eventually consume us all. As the old spiritual says, "God gave Noah the rainbow sign, no more water, the fire next time."

This means, in our terms, the kind of commitment from young people that kept the South in ferment in the heady days of the early 1960's. It is the kind of commitment that may take over the dean's office one day, but then the welfare office the next; the kind of commitment that will mean year-round participation in a new politics, a people's politics, a politics that will insure a choice, and not just an echo, at the top of the ballot.

And it will require that each of us keep in mind a prophecy written by the late Langston Hughes—that dreams deferred do explode. For if this dream is deferred much longer, then an explosion certainly will come.

Du Bois later enlarged his remark—that the problem of the twentieth century would be the problem of the color line—to include the problem of the have-nots pitted against the haves.

Sixty-five years ago, he wrote a personal credo that if adopted by those in power would be a beginning in the struggle to eliminate the problem:

I believe in God who made of one blood all races that dwell on earth. I believe that all men, black and brown and white, are brothers, varying, through Time and Opportunity, in form and gift and feature, but differing in no essential particular, and alike in soul and in the possibility of infinite development.

Especially do I believe in the Negro race; in the beauty of its genius, the sweetness of its soul, its strength in that meekness which shall inherit this turbulent earth . . .

I believe in the Prince of Peace. I believe that War is Murder. I believe that armies and navies are at bottom the tinsel and braggadocio of oppression and wrong; and I believe that the wicked conquest of weaker and darker nations by nations white and stronger but foreshadows the death of that strength.*

* W. E. B. Du Bois, in Darkwater, *Voices from Within the Veil*. Harcourt, Brace & Howe, New York, 1920.

I-
The People Next Door

MY CONSTITUENTS are almost all black, nearly 95 per cent of them. My district, House District 111, is in urban Atlanta, within sight of the new soaring downtown banks and office buildings constructed during the 1960's. But my constituents do not share in that affluence. They are nearly all poor—their average yearly income per family is $2,500. They have trouble finding work—unemployment in my district runs between 30 and 40 per cent. They are poorly educated—on the average they have completed only the sixth grade.

Most of the men in particular have trouble finding work, and so the labor force in my district is predominantly female. These women do the kind of work poorly educated black women do—daywork, domestic service, cleaning someone else's kitchen, caring for someone else's children or for old people.

Incidentally, the few white citizens of my district share the same condition, but unfortunately for them, most of them think—with perhaps some justice—that the color of their skin makes their small amount of money go farther, or that their whiteness makes their poor sixth-grade education better than the one my black constituents have.

These statistics simply demonstrate that my constituents are probably very much like other urban blacks. They are poor, and they depend on government, very largely on their city and county and state governments as well as their federal government, to help them do the things they are unable to do for themselves.

That is why they have chosen a black man to represent them. They still retain some faith in the power of the democratic process to solve people's problems.

I am very afraid that in the past several years they have suffered many disappointments.

They were like most other black Americans in another thing—they voted very heavily for Hubert Humphrey in 1968. They wanted him to be President of the United States. They may have had another first choice, but that was denied them by an assassin in Los Angeles. They may even have had, as I did, a second choice, but that was denied them by the brand of democracy practiced at the Democratic convention in Chicago.

So, they voted for Mr. Humphrey. He represented warmth, while one can find only coldness in the iciness we have since heard described as the "new" Nixon.

So while they were voting one way, much of the rest of the country voted another, either for Nixon or for the third-party brand of even less subtle racism. The democratic process chose a man who said he didn't expect to get black votes, and therefore never sought them out; it chose a man who said publicly he was for open housing but said privately that he was against it; and it chose a man who said the federal government was enforcing the 1954 Supreme Court school desegregation decision too swiftly.

The man in the White House has tremendous power to set either a positive or a negative future for black Americans. He may yet choose a total of five or six or more Supreme Court justices, and therefore may determine the kind of decisions the court makes in civil rights cases over the rest of this century.

His attorney general, head of the U.S. Department of Justice, has been in a position to decide how vigorously—or whether at all —legislation that affects black people most directly is enforced.

The President has named staff and set budgets for the Department of Health, Education, and Welfare, the Department of Housing and Urban Development, and the Office of Economic Opportunity. He has determined how these agencies respond when they are asked to deal with problems of the black and the poor. He may yet have a great deal to say about the nature of the next Congress, and perhaps about the next four years of executive leadership in this country (a grim thought).

Those are not the kinds of decisions one wants to leave to a man whose closest advisers still include Senator Strom Thurmond of South Carolina.

The 1968 Presidential election left us to be governed by a man who was not the choice of 90 per cent of American blacks, and who has yet to demonstrate that he has any concern for the poor or the black. We are ruled by a man who says he wants to rebuild our slums with black capitalism, which at best can only mean exchanging exploiters of one race for those of another.

Having experienced that kind of government over the past three years plus, the way that all of us act in the immediate future, from now until November 1972, is going to be very important.

Because we face the possibility of four more such years. We face, possibly, a Congress that will be more conservative than the present one. We face a nation that has grown tired of the demands of the black and the poor, who are worse off, relatively speaking, than several years ago.

The statistics that show more black people working, more living in decent homes, more getting an education, more earning more money, are well known.

But there is another set of figures that show black people make less money now. More in comparison with what we used to make, but less in comparison with white people. We are moving out of poverty, but while white poverty in America has decreased 27 per cent, black poverty has decreased only 3 per cent.

The most frightening figure is this one. The infant mortality rate for blacks—compared with whites—was 70 per cent higher in

1940. In other words, black babies died 70 per cent more often than white babies did. There had been some change by the 1960's, however, when that comparative figure reached 90 per cent—90 per cent higher infant mortality among black children.

Now, in addition even to these kinds of problems, we have faced and lived through and still are involved in a problem of national proportions, a problem that has affected every American, black and white. That problem is America's imperial war in Vietnam. The difference between black and white is that it affects black people more.

The war in Vietnam has fed on the black community. It has taken our sons and fathers and brothers and uncles to fight and die in it in greater proportion than any other group of Americans. Is that because we are braver or because we love fighting more than anyone else or because we are greater patriots? I think not. I think it is because young black men find the Army uniform and three square meals a day often more attractive than they find life in Harlem or Watts or the Delta of Mississippi or the bayous of Louisiana.

And so the war has taken them in wholesale lots. It sent them eight thousand miles away from their homes, telling them they were defending freedom, the kind of freedom they often find lacking in the communities they left behind. The war placed many young black men in an integrated situation for the first time—a frontline foxhole, next to some white boy—though America has not yet discovered how to get that kind of integration at home.

Most of us have been spectators to the war.

We have watched the young black man and the white boy on television, often in living color, as they burn down the huts of some poor Vietnamese village, and realize the two of them could not live on the same block in most American villages. We must realize further that a young black boy lucky enough to survive the war may come home and may become so frustrated at the discrimination and racism he meets in the land of his birth that he may burn down some American village, using, of course, the skills and the techniques he learned while defending America's freedom overseas.

Many blacks have believed that the war didn't affect them, that it was at least not a primary concern, that it was a foreign policy matter, and that we ought not say anything about it, that it wasn't our business.

Anytime anyone lives in a country that is willing to pay $500,-000 for every enemy soldier it kills, and only $50.75 for every poor person in the war on poverty, then that is our business.

If we find ourselves living in a country that tells us violence is all right when it results in death and destruction for some little brown people eight thousand miles away but not when it is done by black people here at home, then it is our business.

Every time our government tells us that the trouble in Vietnam is caused by outside agitators from the North, think back to George Wallace and Lester Maddox telling us that Southern blacks would be happy and satisfied if it weren't for the outside agitators from the American North.

We have to make it our business to tackle the twin evils of twentieth-century Americanism—racism and militarism.

Black people could begin to do that by making our own communities strong, and by controlling the goods and services and the institutions of our communities. For a long time, in the black community, we have had only the church. That was the only thing that was ours, and ours alone. But I hope in the future that we will begin to widen our sights, and say to ourselves that if anything operates in a black community, black people have got to control it.

That means the businesses and it means the schools and it may mean the police as well.

In New York City I once visited Intermediate School 201. That is one of the Harlem schools that is controlled and run by a neighborhood. Speaking to a class of eighth graders, I mentioned some prominent black people who have come from Georgia, and with

Roy Hamilton and Ray Charles and James Brown and Otis Redding and Gladys Knight and the Pips I mentioned the Honorable Elijah Muhammad. Now one may not think that eighth graders ought to be taught about Ray Charles or James Brown, and maybe you don't think that Elijah Muhammad is a proper subject for an eighth-grade class either, but they knew who he was. One eighth grader told me, "Elijah Muhammad taught racist doctrines and that's why Malcolm X left the Muslims." Another told me that, "The Honorable Elijah Muhammad is the leader of the Nation of Islam and the Messenger of Allah."

Now I submit that that's a wonderful thing—not that one child agrees with Mr. Muhammad and another does not, but that both know about him, and both know he is a part of our peculiar history in the United States.

I think black people have got to be aware of and suspicious of attempts to turn us against our own interests. Take Mr. Nixon's black capitalism, for instance. As he explains it, black capitalism means that General Motors will be given tax credits to come into my community to set up a factory that will hire and train black people. Now that is wonderful, but it is not black capitalism by any stretch of the imagination. That is white capitalism once again coming into the black community and taking the only thing we have to offer, which is our labor.

Instead, we ought to become interested in forms of community socialism. We ought to be interested in the kind of economic development in our communities that will not only give us jobs, but will give the community the profit as well.

We are also going to have to look around us for the kinds of people we can join forces with. It would be nice if we could go it alone. I am sure there is not a single black American who hasn't said to himself, at one time or another, "I wish I could just get away from all this." But we can't, and our numbers are so small nationally that we have got to find the kinds of people who can help us. Those we used to depend on have deserted us. Organized labor used to call itself our friend but you saw where much of the labor vote was in the 1968 Presidential election. Maybe it was not surprising in light of many unions' racist and restrictive hiring practices.

White liberals and moderates used to help us too, but the war in Vietnam pretty well distracted them and attracted nearly all their attention.

So we have got to try to find new friends, while we hope the old ones will come home. We naturally ought to look to the other colored minorities, Chicanos and native Americans. And if we could get any kind of response through the heavy shield of racism that blinds poor white people, they would be our natural allies too.

So, we have to always be on the lookout for any other forces in American political society that can help us, can help my constituents, the poor and the black. We ought not to turn anyone down. If your house is on fire and a man runs up with a bucket of water, don't ask him where he got it or who he is, just make sure it's not gasoline and then pour it on.

Finally, although we need fast action, we have to move with care. We are living in strange times. In 1968, for the first time in more than a decade, the forces of racial conservatism won a national election. In that same election, for the first time since 1948, we had a Presidential candidate who openly appealed to racism. In that year, the hillbilly Hitler from Alabama won almost ten million votes. In 1972, he is back again, and we must be ready for him. We live in an era in which the Vice-President of the United States makes jokes about Polacks and Japs—you know that any man who does that will also joke about wops and spics and niggers too. We live in an era in which a member of the U.S. House of Representatives can remark publicly on the possibility of establishing concentration camps like those the Japanese were put in during the Second World War. But this time they don't mean to put the Japanese in them. They intend them for black Americans.

In an era like that, we ought to consider that an attack on one of us is really an attack on all of us.

We ought to remember what a German minister had to say when someone asked him what he did to stop Hitler from coming to power. "In Germany they first came for the Communists and I didn't speak up because I wasn't a Communist," said Pastor Martin Niemöller. "Then they came for the Jews, and I didn't speak up because I wasn't a Jew. Then they came for the trade unionists, and I didn't speak up because I wasn't a trade unionist. Then they came for the Catholics, and I didn't speak up because I was a Protestant. Then they came for me—and by that time no one was left to speak up."

I have believed that black Americans are and will continue to be a great people because we come from a great people. We have great heroes. But a people with a limited view of their own past will have a limited future. Consider one short passage that comes from the past, from Frederick Douglass.

His words of one hundred years ago still apply today:

He who would be free must strike the first blow. You know that liberty given is never so precious as liberty sought for and fought for. The man who is outraged is the man who must make the first outcry. Depend on it, men will not care much for a people who do not care for themselves. Men will organize to prevent cruelty to animals, for they are dumb creatures, and cannot speak for themselves, but we are men, and men must speak for themselves or we shall not be spoken for at all. We hold it self evident that no class or color should be the exclusive rulers of this country. If there is such a ruling class, there must of course be a subject class, and when that condition is established, the government of the people, by the people and for the people will perish from the earth.

II-

A Little Political History

I HAVE GIVEN a good deal of thought to the experiences of black people in the South in American politics. Our history in this art is not a long one, but it has some glorious chapters. Our politics properly begins just over one hundred years ago, in 1868.

That was the year W. E. B. Du Bois was born. That was the year Hampton Institute opened in Virginia. And it was the year after Morehouse College in Georgia, Howard University in Washington, D.C., and Talladega College in Alabama all first opened their doors. It was the year in which the Fourteenth Amendment became a part of the United States Constitution. It was a year in which America suffered some race riots.

It was a year in which the South Carolina Constitutional Convention met in Charleston, with 124 delegates; 76 of those delegates were black.

The next nine years began to put black people exactly where we are today.

In 1870, a black man was on the South Carolina Supreme Court. A black man, Hiram R. Revels, born in North Carolina, succeeded Jefferson Davis as a United States senator representing Mississippi, the first black man in Congress. The so-called Ku Klux Klan Acts were introduced and passed in Congress, putting Southern elections in the hands of federal officials and guaranteeing the civil and political rights of the newly freed black men through the federal courts and at the point of a gun.

A black man named Robert Wood was elected mayor of Natchez, Mississippi, and a man named Joseph H. Rainey of South Carolina was sworn in as the first black man in the United States House of Representatives.

In 1872, P. B. S. Pinchback, a black man, became acting governor of Louisiana. The next year, 1873, Pinchback was elected to the United States Senate but was never seated. Henry E. Hayne, a black man who served as secretary of state of South Carolina, enrolled at the University of South Carolina.

Two years later, in 1875, a civil rights bill was enacted by Congress. It gave black people the right to equal treatment in inns, on public conveyances, in theaters and other places of public amusement.

A Virginia-born black man, Blanche Kelso Bruce, entered the United States Senate to represent Mississippi, and subsequently became the first of his race to serve a full term in that body.

But by 1875 things had begun to regress. There had been riots staged by white men, assassinations, massacres, and intimidation of black voters. The governor of Mississippi asked for federal troops to protect black voters; the request was refused. That year, conservatives won in the state's general elections, and other states, particularly South Carolina and Louisiana, were quick to adopt legal segregation, or what became known as the Mississippi Plan.

Two years later, in a hotel in Washington, oddly enough a hotel owned by a black man, as historian Lerone Bennett recounts, representatives of President-to-be Rutherford B. Hayes and representatives of the South signed an agreement that, in their own words, gave to the people of the South "the right to control their own affairs in their own way."

This was in February 1877. Two months later, federal troops were withdrawn from cities in South Carolina and Louisiana. Less than four years later, Tennessee began the strange career of Jim Crow by passing a law that required segregation in railroad cars. In less than forty years, every other Southern state had done the same, and more.

Black Americans have seen their political fortunes rise and ebb more than once. They have seen political promises made and broken in Washington. From the days when Frederick Douglass said, "The Republican party is the ship; all else is the sea," to the days of Franklin Delano Roosevelt, black people have tried first one and now the other national political party. They have been ill served by politicians whom the late Ralph McGill, publisher of the Atlanta *Constitution,* once called "so grotesque it seems impossible they could have been influential."

But those nine years just after 1868 were the years—short in number, uneven and irregular—in which American democracy meant the same thing in Mississippi for black people as it always has in Maine for white people.

Now we find ourselves in a similar period. Rutherford B. Hayes ended the first Reconstruction in Washington in the Wormley Hotel in 1877. Richard Nixon has been trying to strangle the short-lived second Reconstruction ever since he made his deal in a Miami Beach hotel in 1968.

Of course the second Reconstruction and the first were not exactly alike. That first one began with the ending of the Civil War. This one we are watching disappear now had several beginnings: the close of the Second World War, when black men came home from Europe determined to die here, if need be, for what many had died for over there; the Montgomery bus boycott in 1956, when a young black minister introduced a new technique into the struggle of black people; the 1960 sit-ins, when young black, and some white, college students showed a determination that their elders were lacking; the 1965 Voting Rights Act, when we in the South thought that freedom, like the end of the war in Vietnam, was "just around the corner."

All these beginnings began to abort in Miami Beach in 1968. They didn't end because one political party left power and another took over; because one man lost and another won; life is not that simple. But they ended because of a combination of circumstances and people and events that made it possible for the forces of evil to conspire, and because the forces of good were, as they nearly always are, powerless and divided. These made possible the political adultery between the incumbent President and South Carolina's Senator Thurmond.

Most American white people apparently believe that since black people can now vote in some places where we couldn't before, can sit in the front of buses that never used to stop, can go to schools that were formerly closed, that life is fine with black Americans.

The result of that feeling, and the corresponding but opposite feeling of black people that bus rides are useless if you have no place to go, lunch-counter seats are useless if you can't afford a meal, votes are useless if you have to choose between a Wallace, a Maddox, an Eastland, and others of that lot, was that these two forces clashed. After the explosions—in Watts, in Newark, in Detroit—we came out the loser.

You could see that feeling demonstrated as law and order became the popular slogan of the day.

You can see it demonstrated when white political candidates in city after city after city get elected because they promise to put down "crime in the streets." The most recent notable example came in November 1971 when Philadelphia elected as mayor a man whose chief public image was that of being a "tough cop," a man who talks of a local-option version of capital punishment.

You can see it operating when the United States Department of Justice takes a back seat in the school integration struggle; when the Nixon Administration proposes a voting rights bill that would reduce the number of registered black voters; and when the nine old men who used to be our last hope and court of last appeal are steadily whittled away.

We from the South have come a long way since 1868, much of it an unhappy way. We have seen black men in high places removed, and we have begun the slow struggle back to the top again.

Our next push must be to seize control not just of the county courthouse and city hall as our brothers in Alabama and Mississippi have done in a few cases, but of the halls of Congress as well. From the twenty-six heavily black congressional districts in the South, there are sure to be black candidates in 1972 and in 1974. Some of these will falter, but some will win.

A year after the 1968 Presidential election, I worked for a time with the Voter Education Project of the Southern Regional Council interviewing black candidates. In talking with such men and women, you discover what the experience of politics has meant to black Southerners.

I asked Lucius Amerson, the sheriff of Macon County, Alabama, why he thought he won his election. "I won," he said, "because I had determination and because the people knew I could bring a better day in Macon County as far as law enforcement and protection go."

Mrs. Geneva Collins, the Chancery Clerk of Claiborne County, Mississippi, was asked what her election meant to black people in her area. "It seemed," she said, "to give the Negro race the feeling they had made the first step toward overcoming discrimination, poverty and neglect in every area. They feel like they can progress."

I asked Eddie Davis, now a police juror (or county commissioner) in West Feliciana Parish in Louisiana, why he ran for office. "We had no voice in the courthouse," said Mr. Davis. "We didn't have a voice in anything we undertook to do. All days were the white man's day; the Negroes had no voice in anything. We just had to do what the white man said. I made up my mind that whenever I got in power, got to be a registered voter, I would run for election. After I registered and voted, there came up an election, and I decided I would run for something. It didn't make any difference what it was; if it was something I could manage, I was going to run, whether I won or lost. I was doing it to let the white man know that the Negroes wanted their rights. Not for what I could get out of it, I wasn't running for that. I was running to develop my race, so I decided to run."

I talked to Charles Evers, the mayor of Fayette, Mississippi, after his unsuccessful race for Congress, a historic contest in which he ran first in the primary but lost in a runoff election. Since then Evers made new history for Mississippi by running for governor. I asked Evers what significance he thought that congressional campaign had had and what effect it would have in the future.

"I think it was one of the greatest things you could mention," he said. "It gave Negroes hope, because for a while Negroes believed that the vote didn't count . . . it inspired Negroes to become involved in politics. And it is going to help elect Negroes and change that rotten system.

"Don't become a racist. Talk about the issues and the problems of the Negroes and what you are going to do to change them. Once you are elected, don't turn white and forget the Negro . . . if Negroes can get together they can control and rule something. My feeling is that Negroes have got to control something in America . . .

"My advice is to control something, control the economics of the county, control the ballot of the county, the politics of the county . . .

"We don't holler black power . . . but watch it."

III-

Revolution on Campus

IN THE TWENTIETH-CENTURY United States, the consciousness of the schooled and unschooled is occupied more and more
with the question of what the university should be or do.

The crisis of race that exists on the college campus is only a
reflection of a larger, more serious crisis in the country and, indeed,
throughout the world. I've already mentioned what I believe to be
the roots of the crisis: the continuing failure of the white minority
of peoples of this world to share power and wealth with the nonwhite majority.

That this crisis should come to the college campus is natural;
here, after all, are the people who have been told since the day
they graduated from high school that the earth is theirs for the
taking, that they are the inheritors of tomorrow. Who is to blame
if they believe it? That this feeling has spread downward into high
schools and even elementary schools is not surprising either.

It ought not be surprising that young people who learned how
to organize the poor and powerless in the Mississippi Delta would
transfer their expertise to the powerless at Berkeley and Cornell.
And it ought not be surprising that race has played a large part
in the continuing struggle of man against man. To tie campus

31

unrest only to yesterday's off-campus protests is unreal, however. There is much more at stake than that.

A great deal has been made by some scholars and pollsters of the difference in the demands of black and white student activists. The white students want revolution, the experts say, while all the blacks want—despite their revolutionary rhetoric—is reform, a chance to bend the established system to their own ends, which are as safe and as ordinary as those they share with the rest of middle-class America.

A dangerous conflict is present in the black mind on the American campus. The black student is torn between the need for a regular, formal education, part of the socialization process that we are told everyone needs in order to seek an acceptable role in society, and his need to carve out a new education experience, one that is meaningful to him as a black person.

A young girl who was a student at Tougaloo College in Mississippi summed up this feeling when she heard that Tougaloo and Brown University had entered into an educational compact, with Brown acting as big brother.

We argued that Tougaloo could do better [she wrote], that we did not have to pattern ourselves after Brown or any of the Ivy League schools, that we had a unique opportunity to make Tougaloo a revolutionary institute of learning. We questioned the notion that places like Brown offered a superior education; we felt in fact that they dealt in mis-education. We felt that if schools like Brown had been truly educating their students then the state of the country and the world would be a lot different.*

The dilemma of whether to concentrate on transforming the Tougaloos of the world or to get what we can from the Browns is a continuing one among young blacks. The demand for a black dorm or an Afro-American center is a part of this dilemma. The

* Arverna Adams, *Wilson Library Bulletin,* September 1968.

unscholarly attacks on black educational institutions by white scholars who should know better are part of that dilemma.

So the current and future course for those blacks interested in solving—or rather eliminating—the crisis of race is unclear. On the one hand it is educated and civilized man who has put us where we are today. The rape of Vietnam was not begun by high-school dropouts, but by liberally educated men. The pollution of the air and water is not carried out by fools and idiots, but by men educated at the best scientific and technical centers. The ability to shape a society that spends nearly $100 billion on conquering space and dominating the globe militarily comes from men of genius, supposedly, men capable of governing nations, not from men who have had limited opportunities.

And yet while these struggles of the twentieth century continue, the university has tended in some ways to remain aloof, a center for the study of why man behaves as he does, but never a center for the study of how to make man behave in a civilized manner.

Robert M. Hutchins, former chancellor of the University of Chicago, has described the present-day university thusly:

[It was hoped that the modern university] would lead the way to national power and prosperity . . . become the central factory of the knowledge industry, the foundation of our future. [Instead, it became] the national screening device through which individuals were to be put in the proper productive relationship to the national program of power and prosperity.

[But] the world has moved too fast for the university. The leaders of the younger generation see that the problem is not to get wealth and power; [nations] have enough of those already. The problem is justice, or what to do with wealth and power. An institution that evidently has little interest in this question cannot command the allegiance of the young.*

* Robert M. Hutchins, "The Constitution of Public Education," *The Center Magazine*, July 1969.

It is evident that the allegiance of some of the young is not with the university but with the oppressed and downtrodden. Every continent has seen its young rise up against the evils the university is supposed to teach them how to destroy, and many have risen up against the university itself.

Despite its record of producing individuals who know their relationship to power and prosperity and are prepared to be the managers of the new industrial and technological society, the university has happily, and probably against its wishes, produced a new crop of activists whose demands on the university will, one hopes, be expanded to include assaults on the foundations of a society that has perverted education to reinforce inequity. The entire fabric of education is being attacked. All black students have done is to have allowed their demands to be colored by their special situation.

Why should we not demand amnesty, the young ask, when you have allowed yourselves amnesty for more than three hundred years? Why should we negotiate, they ask, when you have received your own personal amnesty since you came to power?

Why should we not use weapons, when you have used them time and time again against us?

Why should we be accused of tearing down the university and having nothing to put in its place, when you have torn down Vietnam and left the ghetto standing?

Why should we not have a black house on campus, the blacks ask, when the Methodists, Episcopalians, Jews, and Catholics often have theirs?

Why shouldn't we take over a building and evict the deans; isn't every big-city university, in connivance with urban renewal, doing the same thing to entire families every day?

Why should we not learn about ourselves, the blacks ask. Haven't we been made to learn more than we ever wanted to know about white America?

Why shouldn't any and every black high-school graduate be admitted freely to this college, the blacks ask. Aren't they being taught by your graduates, and therefore shouldn't they have learned what it takes to fit in here?

Why should Dow Chemical or ROTC be on campus? the students ask. We are not here to learn to make napalm or to learn how to be soldiers. This is not a vocational school for *any* employer. Or at least it should not be.

This ought to be, the students say, a center for the shaping of civilized man; a center for the study of not just why man behaves as he does, but also a place to study how to make him behave better.

To do this, the university must rid itself of old notions. Higher education can no longer be regarded as a privilege for a few, but must be seen as a right for the many. None of the rhetoric of the past several years about an education for everyone really approaches this aim; higher education is still an elitist and largely white preserve in America today.

In an age when the nature of education itself is being questioned, to permit or even to require that everyone receive a piece of parchment that will establish that he knows what millions of people already know with little profit to mankind will not do. It is simply not enough.

What is it then that is lacking? What is there beyond four years of compressing some of the world's knowledge from lecture notes to the little blue books?

For the blacks, it must be more than Swahili lessons and Afro-American centers, although these have their place. For white universities, it must be more than raiding Southern black schools and taking their most talented faculty and students. For the black school, it must be more than pride in blackness. It must be, for all, the development not just of curriculum but an ideology suited to extricate man from his history.

A writer in *The Center Magazine,* Peter Marin, has offered a gloomy view of the university's failing function:

Students are encouraged to relinquish their own wills, their freedom of volition; they are taught that value and culture reside outside oneself, and must be acquired from the institutions, and almost everything in their education is designed to discourage them from activity, from the wedding of idea and act. It is almost as if we hoped to discourage them from thought itself, by making ideas so lifeless, so hopeless, that their despair would be enough to make them manipulable and obedient.*

While the university may have bred despair, luckily it has not succeeded in breeding obedience. Violence occurs where there is no politics. While there is no politics of race, or rather while there is no anti-racist politics at the university level, violence—physical and intellectual—will flourish.

Until the university develops a politics—or in perhaps more academic terms, a curriculum and a discipline that stifles and eliminates war and poverty and racism—until then, the university will be in doubt.

If education is a socializing process, it has in our society prepared white people to continue enjoying privileged traditions and positions, while black people have been programmed for social and economic oblivion. Today's black and white students see this. They see the university become hospitable to war and to directing counterrevolutions. Its professors are employed in the Pentagon. Its presidents serve on commission after commission investigating and recommending last year's solutions to the last century's problems. The universities recruit ghetto students with substandard backgrounds and then subject these students to the standards of white middle-class America.

They believe, as does the Tougaloo student I quoted earlier, that:

the task for black students and black Americans is much greater than trying to change white institutions and their white counter-

* Peter Marin, "The Open Truth and the Fiery Vehemence of Youth," *The Center Magazine,* September 1969.

parts in the South. The task is to create revolutionary institutes of learning. The act of trying to be a better person, or trying to imagine and create humane institutions is formidable, but we have no other alternative. We must have a prototype from which to build a good society. The point which I make is an old one: that revolution is not the seizure of power, but is also the building of a society that is qualitatively better than the one we presently live in.*

But perhaps the university's response—and society's response— ought to be closer to sentiments like those of W. E. B. Du Bois, in words written some fifty years ago:

We believe that the vocation of man in a modern, civilized land includes not only the technique of his actual work but intelligent comprehension of his elementary duties as a father, citizen, maker of public opinion . . . a conserver of the public health, an intelligent follower of moral customs, and one who can appreciate if not partake something of the higher spiritual life of the world. We do not pretend that this can be taught to each individual in school, but it can be put into his social environment, and the more that environment is restricted and curtailed the more emphatic is the demand that . . . [man] shall be trained and trained thoroughly in these matters of human development if he is to share the surrounding civilization.†

Or, indeed, if there is to be any civilization at all.

---

* Adams, *op. cit.*
† *Op. cit.* p. 15.

IV-
Killers of the Dream

A HISTORICAL ANALYSIS of the minority experience is familiar to everyone of a certain age and a certain degree of literacy; an economic analysis of the great social cost borne by minority groups is familiar litany to most Americans; the pathology that results from this experience, both in persons and in institutions, is equally familiar to any American who watched Detroit burn or Watts smolder.

The cause of the dismay, this dispossession, this disruption and destruction of the lives of millions of nonwhite Americans, is simple: it is that a country founded by white men more than three hundred years ago has remained in the eyes of its citizens and rulers and subjects a white country today.

John Jay wrote of this nation in *The Federalist,* "Providence has been pleased to give this one connected country to one united people . . . a people descended from the same ancestors, speaking the same language, professing the same religion, attached to the same principles of government, very similar in their manners and customs . . ."

It has been suggested under that philosophy that black men were designed by Providence to work for white men; Indians, unsuited by Providence to be slaves, had to be dispensed with; Mexicans, being neither Indians nor blacks, became cultural enemies who held territory that was manifestly destined for the white man.

But what confuses today's college administrators and city managers and political bosses and well-meaning liberals is their lack of understanding that today's black push is part of the old fight against the kind of white man's Providence that justified slavery and condoned wholesale slaughter of Indians and supported the lust for land owned by Mexicans.

And so this country pretended to democracy and made an institution of racism; the European immigrants who later came here to escape discrimination instilled it in their young.

The history of white Providence must include the history of militant response from its nonwhite victims, a history of resistance, a history of struggle, and a history of separatist movements aimed at getting the white man's foot from the nonwhite man's neck.

From the first days of the founding fathers, we have seen rejection and rebellion against white Providence by nonwhite people here. That rebellion has sometimes been bloody as were the revolts of Denmark Vesey and Nat Turner. It has progressed through oratory, petitions, marches, and peaceful protests, and back in the 60's to blood again.

That history is shared not just by black men, but by red men as well. Listen to a debate between Tecumseh, a Shawnee Indian, and another Indian over which of several ways Indians ought to take to free themselves from white Providence.

"Are we not being stripped, day by day, of the little that remains of our ancient liberty?" demanded Tecumseh. "Do they not even now kick and strike us as they do their blackfaces? How long will it be before they tie us to a post and whip us to make us work in a cornfield as they do them? Shall we wait for that moment or shall we die fighting before we submit to such . . . ?"

As usual, there was a moderate in the crowd. He answered Tecumseh by saying: "Let us submit our grievances, whatever they may be, to the Congress of the United States . . ."

This debate took place in 1812. Neither side seems to have prevailed, if the present-day condition of American Indians is any indication. So, now, at the beginning of the 70's, these same groups —Indians, blacks, Mexicans—are still fighting against white Providence. The argument proposed by Tecumseh still rages in our communities.

It rages because two hundred years after the founding fathers forged a new nation, one that was supposed to represent a melting pot of peoples, the only thing that has not melted is us. Now we no longer quite wish to melt, to be absorbed, to fit in, to join up, to enter into the mainstream. Our job, from now into the future, is to carve out our own place; separate, but a part of the whole.

That can be done partly with tremendous effort on our part. That effort will take dedication from our young people, dedication to the notion that black power, political and economic, must be more than rhetoric. It will take recognition that it is both evil men and an evil system that we deal with, a system that rumbles, beastlike, over our every aspiration. It will take the recognition that this system, representative democracy, has yet to work for us and therefore does not work for the society as a whole.

It has won some small victories. It has won free access to lunch counters, providing potential steak dinners for a people with hotdog pocketbooks. It has won for us the right to sit in the front of the bus, a hollow victory for a people whose only trip is from the feudal South to the mechanized high-rise poverty of the North. It has won the right to vote for a people who have seldom seen a candidate for whom they could honestly vote.

We have to begin to do that by making our own communities as strong as they can be. We have to exercise control over all of the resources and institutions of our community.

Secondly, we have to *get our politics together,* and get together with others, no matter whom they may be, to form flexible alliances.

That means if the labor movement wants something that we want too, then we support labor and labor must support us. It means that if the all-white suburbs join us in supporting opposition to American imperialism abroad, then we join in that struggle too. It does not mean that labor and suburban whites necessarily remain our allies forever. Their interests and ours will not and cannot coincide always, and we must be careful to separate coincidental interest and coalition from foolish submission to strange bed-fellows.

These are ordinary tactics and ought to be carried out by any people.

But, in addition to doing the ordinary things, we ought to consider always and be ready always, for the *extraordinary* things. Extraordinariness, of course, assumes that if regular and responsible and democratic and fair methods don't work for us, then others must be considered.

The possibility of *violent revolution* must not be dismissed, although prospects for it are doubtful at present. It is simply unrealistic to expect that a small percentage of the population, poorly organized and poorly armed, can overthrow a massive government with vast police powers at its disposal.

It is particularly unrealistic when one considers that the winding down of the war in Vietnam, though people are still being killed, brings to an end with it a large part of the white radical movement that might be expected to join in such a revolution. And it is also unrealistic if you consider that those who order society are usually able to keep it stable by allowing minimal reforms so that even oppression becomes bearable.

But one can imagine that that day of revolution may come.

Until or unless it does, however, one ought to work toward building a movement powerful enough to either operate without it or powerful enough to take advantage of the moment when it arrives.

That movement can have many constituent parts, and it ought

to be a political movement. It ought to be political because in 1972 politics for oppressed peoples will cease being the art of compromise and the art of the possible and will begin being the art of seeing who gets how much of what from whom. This political movement will have constituent parts because none of its individual sections is powerful enough to stand alone. It is a movement that will see its constituent groups acting together in one instance and acting alone in others.

And it will be a movement that ought to feel it can draw heavily on the young: those bruised veterans of the 1968 Chicago convention; those who felt rejected and useless after the Meredith March in Mississippi; those who feel that academic life is sterile and irrelevant; those who fought for a losing Presidential candidate and were denied their choice, either by assassination or boss rule, and then saw a man of Richard Nixon's cynical politics and flawed vision enter the White House . . . all those can become organizers for such a movement.

They can help put its parts together. They can help build a machinery powerful enough to take control in a peaceful, orderly fashion, or take control following the example of those who now exercise great power.

Of the late Dr. Martin Luther King, Jr., someone once said, paraphrasing Genesis 37:19–20: "They said one to another, behold, here comes the dreamer, let us slay him and we shall see what will become of his dreams."

Those who refuse to take action are killers of the dream. They have slain too many dreamers, and will be adding the murder of hope to their death list.

But if we put this new political force together, then we can build the kind of world the silent Statue of Liberty seems to be seeking as she stands in New York harbor and asks:

> *Give me your tired, your poor,*
> *Your huddled masses yearning to breathe free,*

The wretched refuse of your teeming shore,
*Send these, the homeless, tempest-tossed, to me. . . .**

Sweetheart, here we are!

---

* Emma Lazarus, "The New Colossus: Inscription for the Statue of Liberty, New York Harbor."

V-

Black Hands, Black Sweat

WE LIVE in the United States in a largely white male-dominated business world. As black people today go in quest of ways and means to achieve economic stability, we find ourselves groping with many questions that will directly affect our people and communities in the 1970's.

The questions that most affect our lives are the ones that have been created from the day the first white man set foot on what he was to call America. From that day to this we have been treated as if we were only living and surviving at his pleasure and discretion. We have never been allowed to enjoy the comforts that we built for him.

Our position was best described more than a hundred years ago by a black Georgian, Henry M. Turner, who in 1868, trying to describe the condition of black Georgians of his era, accurately describes our economic position now.

"We have pioneered a civilization here," said Turner. "We have built up your country. We have worked in your fields, we have gathered your harvests, for two hundred and fifty years . . . we, who number hundreds of thousands . . . have not a foot of land to call our own. We are strangers in the land of our birth, without money, without education, without aid, without a roof to cover us while we live or clay to cover us when we die."

It could be argued that conditions have improved just a bit since then, but practically, things are still pretty much the same.

Housing, employment, and education, all the things necessary to build whole communities, have been denied us. The white American rose up once to defeat the British in 1776 and free himself from taxation without representation. It is a shame that we have not been inspired to fight a similar battle over taxes ourselves, for if any group pays a heavy penalty—both financially and spiritually—for mere survival in the American welfare state, it is us.

Not only have we had to build the railroads, houses, and schools, but we have had to serve the white American his food, nurse his children, and fight his wars. Indeed, the last 350 years for black people have been no crystal stair. Our sweat and toil in America have been unlike that any other ethnic group has experienced. And among them, we have been under more undue strain and pressure than any other Americans to pull ourselves up, though lacking the base that other ethnic groups (white) had to secure economic and political power.

The ladders of upward financial mobility open to the voluntary immigrants who came to these shores seeking freedom from oppression are closed to us, America's single group of involuntary arrivals. The European American drew his strength from his ability to retain and draw from his European culture, while the African American saw his culture, language, religion, and family destroyed. As legal slavery passed, we entered into a permanent period of unemployment and underemployment from which we have yet to emerge, while the European newcomer found the growth of mercantile capitalism especially fitted to his cashbox mentality.

We have had to endure physical and verbal abuse, take hand-me-down housing, raggedy pawnshop furniture, third- and fourth-hand schoolbooks, debilitated automobiles for transporation, and spend exorbitant bus, train, and subway fares to get to jobs that never provided dignity or decent wages when we got to them. Yet we are told still we have to pull ourselves up by our bootstraps. This is a cruel suggestion for a people without any boots at all.

But we survived. We wear our battle scars proudly and we continue to move to mobilize our people to obtain the right to a decent life where our culture, our beauty, our soul can be reflected in the kinds of ways necessary to make our communities whole and financially stable.

Moving in this direction we must begin taking advantage of what is available to us. We should not single out any one method or way to make ourselves free. But we need to understand the mind of this nation, which is controlled by less than 1 per cent of its population. We have to be clear in our minds when we call down the power structure. We have to know exactly what we mean and what kind of power we can grasp to change it.

The economic power structure of the United States is extremely political. One of the best examples is tne fact that industries that are supposed to be regulated by various government agencies in fact control those agencies.

The Federal Communications Commission does not regulate broadcasting; it looks after the vested interests of broadcasters, routinely renewing radio and television licenses and denying challenges to those public licenses from individuals and groups who are thus locked out of the opportunity to broadcast on the public airways. The Federal Trade Commission is known as a cowardly bureaucratic body that caters to consumer industries instead of protecting the consumers. And so on down the line—the Interstate Commerce Commission serves the railroad and trucking industries; the Federal Aviation Administration acts as the tool of the airline interests. The Agriculture Department pursues racist policies and hands over billions to six thousand corporate farmers not to grow food. The Defense Department grants $50 billion annually to underwrite corporate aircraft giants to make mistakes with C-5A's and pads the pocketbooks of former Pentagon generals. The Justice Department observes monopolistic enterprise and the major gambling syndicates and does nothing, yet persecutes Black Panthers and other black people who dare speak up for their rights.

Given our history of oppression, and the current and past climate of repression of black people, with the might of government aimed at protecting the power of the few who *have* against the many who *have not,* with an official United States economic policy of socialism and welfare millionairism for the wealthy and capitalism and free enterprise for the poor, it is no wonder that economic development must stand high on our list of priorities.

Another thing must be noted. We may be witnessing the beginnings of a totalitarian state not only for black people but for all Americans. As in George Orwell's prophetic *Nineteen Eighty-Four,* the first steps are being taken by the destruction of privacy and the subversion of the English language. As in *Nineteen Eighty-Four,* large segments of the population are becoming so accustomed to oppression that they are no longer shocked by it. The assassination and imprisonment of dissenters are becoming routines of American life.

"Doublethink," the process of confusing words until they mean their opposites, seemed fanciful when Orwell wrote his classic. The present Administration has turned fancy into everyday reality.

"Freedom" is killing Vietnamese in order to make them "free," destroying villages to "free" them (an American officer in Vietnam said: "We had to destroy the village in order to save it."); arming fascist dictatorships in Greece and Cambodia to keep the Greek and Cambodian people "free"; and exploiting the resources and peoples of whole continents in the name of "free" trade.

"Peace" means vast preparations for nuclear war, the expansion of the Vietnam war into Cambodia and Laos and all of Southeast Asia, the stifling of nonviolent protest, and "wasting" lives to win wars that were lost before they were begun.

"Benign" is an adjective that describes a deliberate policy of indifference and neglect.

"Together" is where we bring the people when we call some of them "bums" and "effete snobs."

"Protecting free enterprise" means billions of dollars in subsidies to government contractors, monopolistic corporations, and farmers who don't farm.

The political language of our society is becoming so polluted with "doublethink" and hypocrisy that rational discussion of issues grows steadily more difficult.

What can be done to solve these problems?

Administration spokesmen assure us that violence is not the way, just after they assure us that they will not do anything regardless of what we say in a peaceful nonviolent manner. They assure us that we can get their ear only if we lower our voices, then tell us that millions of nonviolent voices will have no effect on them at all.

Nixon tells black citizens that the business system, not the government, will save us from economic destitution. The business system knows better. A much more candid statement of what business will do under existing circumstances is the following from the editor of *The Bankers Magazine:*

Despite all the exhortations at business symposiums, social and economic threats inherent in racial schism and violence in America have not yet reached the crisis proportions which would make business anti-poverty efforts a vital business need—essential to the continuance of corporate profits, the preservation of capital, or the survival of commerce. As long as this is the case, a major and sustained effort by private business to rehabilitate and normalize the ghetto economy, and bring the ghetto resident into the main economy, will fail since the effort does not fulfill essential corporate needs.*

* Theodore L. Cross, *Black Capitalism*. Atheneum, New York, 1969.

The author of that statement is also the founder of the *Atomic Energy Law Journals,* a director of the Bank Tax Institute, and current chairman of the Banking Law Institute. He is saying very clearly that black people will never have economic freedom unless they muster the force to threaten, counter, or nearly parallel the existence of the entire American economic system. I suspect that if he were black, talk like that would get him thrown into jail, and I am sure he distrusts black people who talk about destroying the economic system that has created his own highly privileged status. But I also suspect that he is right about how far we will have to be prepared to go if we are ever going to be free.

We had better face the situation and get ourselves ready to take care of business, whether it is the kind of business Mr. Cross represents or the kind of humanistic, noncapitalistic business that represents commerce in human relationships, not in dollars and cents.

The question then takes us back to where we as black people want to go. Knowing the odds stacked against us, we have to reach out to our brothers and sisters who have not achieved the economic level that many of us in the middle-to-upper economic brackets have reached.

As Cross says, "The painfully apparent features of the ghetto economy are its economic weakness, a low level of productivity, and the poverty level of its consumers."

Dr. Kenneth Clark's description of the black neighborhood, the ghetto, as a social, educational, political *and* economic colony is especially important to remember.

What we must do, I believe, is to bring positive programming to black people who face similar problems.

For instance, in Alabama, the Southwest Alabama Farmers Cooperative Association is developing land programs and collectively farming the land. Black people now own substantial acreage and are producing needed food and fiber for other black people. Yet little recognition of this program has come from the black businessmen of the Northern, Midwestern or Western cities who are developing their own economic programs to promote black business. These plans, like that presently underwritten by the Honorable Elijah Muhammad in the South, operations that put black people into a healthy and productive relationship with our environment, must receive national support.

We ought to strive toward further collectivization of our economic thrust, so that we do not get caught up in the degrading practice of some of us obtaining all the wealth while our brothers and sisters are still hungry. It is cruel and criminal to have outmoded capitalism thrust upon us, whether dressed in black or under its new, presumably less offensive name, minority entrepreneurship. Capitalism has not solved white people's problems. If it had, engineers in Seattle would not be driving taxicabs today as part of the dislocation and unemployment in the present state of the nation's economy. What black people need is something more properly described as "community socialism"; that would enable a larger share of us to get our hands on the dollars that pass through —and all too often, out of—our own communities. If an economic enterprise does business in our community, we must be more than consumers but must become owners as well.

As much as I despise racketeering, prostitution, and the numbers, if these are to be tolerated by the white-controlled law enforcement agencies that rule this country, then we must own them too. It is too much to prevent us from making even a dishonest dollar in our own community.

In short, we must control what exists where we are. We must always strive for the greatest good for the largest number of us. That means trying to influence General Motors as much as it means trying to take over the corner store, although the first is unlikely and the second may simply change the color of the neighborhood cheats. If the second is done, however, it could lay the foundation for a series of growth steps for us, leading from our store to our farm to our distribution system to what is most important, money in the pockets of our people. If the first is done, and General Motors through some miracle should fall into our hands, it might mean we could build an automobile that would last for more than eighteen months.

If both these adventures are begun, begun seriously with our people in mind and their interests foremost, then something must succeed.

If nothing does and if, as it appears it will, times get harder, then we had better prepare seriously to take care of business ourselves.

VI -

America's Domestic Colony

DR. KENNETH CLARK describes the black ghetto neighborhood as a social, educational, political and economic colony. Let us go further. The United States of America, at the beginning of this decade of the 1970's, is a colonial power, with almost all black citizens being colonial subjects, and almost all white people, willingly or not, consciously or not, colonialists.

The first part of the equation is sure to be disputed by some; the second cannot be. It is supported even by the Kerner Commission Report, the official Establishment statement on the crisis of race in America, which states that "what white Americans have never fully understood—but what the Negro can never forget—is that white society is deeply implicated in the ghetto. White institutions created it, white institutions maintain it, and white society condones it."*

But the colonial status of America's black people has seldom been recognized. It is argued that since blacks in this country are "American" and not "foreign," since we have equal constitutional rights with white people, and since we are not the traditional source

* *Report of the National Advisory Commission on Civil Disorders.* E. P. Dutton, New York, 1968.

52

for raw material and less and less for cheap labor that a colonial people are, then the analysis must be faulty, and the traditional solution to the colonial situation—revolution—is unthinkable here.

It is true that we are American, at least by birth, and partly by language and by culture. When the European immigrant arrived, he gained an immediate—if low-level—economic foothold by providing the unskilled labor needed by industry. The first black immigrants—the slaves—provided needed labor, to be sure, but at no profit to themselves. When the black immigrant finally arrived in the city, he found an already developed economy with little use for him except as a consumer. Even before then, the system of chattel slavery destroyed African cultures and the African family, imposed a strange and alien religion on an already religious people, while the European drew his political and economic strength from the traditions and religion he preserves to this day. As slavery passed, black people entered into a permanent status of underemployment, while the European thrived in an expanding economy and the growing age of entrepreneurial opportunities.

It is certainly a paper fact that black Americans and white Americans enjoy equal constitutional status, at least in popular theory, though some of those rights that every schoolboy knows are guaranteed by the Constitution, like the right to vote, are still the subject of intense argument, not just in the Reconstructed South, but in the halls of Congress as well. And the class position of most black people, complicated and colored by the fact of race in a society dominated politically, economically, and socially by whites, makes the usual constitutional guarantees almost worthless except in certain specific situations. The right to belong to a labor union means little to domestic workers; welfare clients have little to do with rules governing them. The resident of the inner city has no power—except that of force and fear—over the police who occupy his neighborhood.

It is true that black people in America offer no source of raw materials, and increasingly, in a technological and increasingly automated society, no source of cheap labor either, a fact from which only the most terrifying conclusions can be drawn. It can be argued that under the traditional forms of colonialism, the colonized people did not fear genocide because they were needed to make the colonial equation add up for the occupying power. Under this new form of domestic colonialism, when the colonial subjects have become a useless and surplus people, what is to prevent genocide or a new slavery if the ruling powers become too irritated at the slaves' demands?

The single conclusion must be that the solutions that have worked in integrating and assimilating the European into the American mainstream cannot—and some would say should not—be used in the case of American blacks. The processes that elevated the European—hard work, self-help, ethnic identification, political activism, economic separatism, intellectual striving—can at best only marginally improve the conditions of the mass of black people in America.

With these techniques black Americans won the right to be accommodated in public places, to use the franchise in most parts of the country, to sue for equal educational opportunities, to protest injustice peacefully, and to peacefully petition government for a redress of grievances. The latter, the constitutional right, was only recently secured—and then at great cost and then not completely —by black people.

So, white American society has always presented the opportunity for some blacks to rise to positions of influence and affluence, and white society now offers an opportunity for general, if minimal, improvements to be won through traditional channels. But it has not yet shown any indication or willingness to change its three-hundred-fifty-year-old history of exploitation and suppression based on race nor its economic system that has always considered property more important than people.

What further complicates the possibility for change is that the discussion has become so cloudy and unreal. We reached a certain incredible point in the late 1960's when 500,000 American troops were engaged in an imperialist occupation of one small country and the invasion of another, both countries being destroyed by American bombs, napalm, and defoliants, while at home black people were cautioned against the use of "senseless violence." In Latin America, the Alliance for Progress, so much ballyhooed a decade ago, has resulted in an increasing flow of dollars from South American client states to the United States, and similar schemes, under the guise of corporate liberalism, are being touted for the American ghettos.

In those nations where it is thought American imperial interests are threatened, particularly Vietnam and Cuba, American military might has been demonstrated to be a helpless force in the face of nationalism and the desire of colonial peoples to free themselves. Nevertheless, the same military solutions are tried again and again in the black colony at home, and now on the college campus, with only limited success.

School bussing, an old practice in virtually each of the fifty states, has become in the mouth of the President of the United States a strange, alien, and un-American practice, "forced bussing," calculated to destroy the child's psyche and the most sacred of all American concepts, the neighborhood school.

The theoretical basis upon which most of public higher education in America is constructed, open admissions, becomes in the sour mouth of the Vice-President of the United States an anti-elitist practice that will destroy the value of an academic degree. Picking up beer cans from the highway is touted as proper social activism by the Nixon Administration, while the corporate murderers who manufacture filth to poison our air and water go free.

The demands of black people who by necessity turn away from democratic procedures—when such procedures are absent or nonfunctional—are called anarchy. In an earlier, prerevolutionary America, looters, rioters, and the destroyers of private property were called patriots, and school children today memorize poems about their exploits. Law and order have become the platitudes of the day, while corporate executives conspire to deliver faulty parts for American military airplanes.

The tragedy in the United States, in regard to this nation's relation to her colonial subjects, both here and abroad, is that we have always chosen the safety of the present order rather than the risks of action and reform.

That is the history of our involvement in Vietnam, where brutal anti-democratic—but, importantly from the American perspective, anti-Communist—regimes are supported, and that is the history at home, where reformist efforts are at the last minute always halted when order is threatened. Could there be a more graphic example than our continued support of a dictator in South Vietnam, even after the farce of a pretend election, an election in which the dictator, our ally, prevented any other candidates from running against him?

So, we are citizens, we black Americans, only in the narrow sense that we must meet certain obligations to the state, without receiving all of the corresponding benefits of citizenship. We all pay taxes, but because more of us are poor, and because the poor pay proportionately more, and because some of the rich pay nothing at all, we pay more of our share for fewer of the rewards taxpayers rightfully expect. Black and white men alike are subjected to the opportunity to serve their country militarily. But throughout the last decade, during the continuing attack by our country on the people of Southeast Asia, young black American men managed to become first in war, last in peace, and seldom in the hearts of our countrymen.

Most immigrants came voluntarily, seeking freedom and a chance to survive. Our ancestors came in chains, husband torn from wife, child from mother.

In a land where family and education are highly venerated, we were denied the chance to learn and to maintain a stable family unit. In a country settled by the victims of religious persecution, we found a strange and alien religion forced upon us. While we came from a land whose inhabitants believed in communalism and the extended family, we found created here a system of mercantile capitalism.

From that day to this, the separate status of black people in the United States has been a fact of life. From that day to this, we have been the colonial Africans, suffering at the hands of the settler Europeans.

We live and work in situations provided for by the majority, not by us. We exist at the pleasure and sufferance of the American majority, and the evidence is mounting that that existence itself may soon be called into question. Part of the difficulty is that the traditional solutions to the ethnic dilemma—solutions employed with great success by other ethnic groups—will not mold themselves entirely to our deliverance.

Individual entrepreneurship has created a class of black millionaires in publishing, insurance, and the cosmetic fields, but has done little for the economic uplift of the mass of black people. Pressure-group politics has won many needed reforms for our group, but it is nearly impossible to make these reforms secure in a colonial society.

We believed, for instance, that the battle for the integrated schoolroom was won in 1954, with only slight pressure needed from then on to finish the job. The truth was that none of the Administrations in Washington since then, particularly this present one, ever intended to make the dream of an integrated education a reality. The traditional coalitions of black people, labor, the more enlightened church leadership, all these have failed in bringing about the beloved society that was the dream of the early 1960's.

At about this time the American labor movement revealed its true interests when black people began to demand not only labor-connected goals like minimum wages, but entry into the craft unions, which have always been lily-white. The churches have all too often played a gadfly, shallow role: interested in black people one day, the war in Vietnam the next, abortion law reform the following week. The hoped-for coalition with white college students has failed to materialize as far too many of this group have shown more interest in music, drugs, the romantic rhetoric of revolution, and the ennobling sacrifice of self-enforced poverty than in the very real problems of day-by-day existence that afflict most black people in this country.

So we are left to the circular route of politics and then protest and then revolt, with the probable result that increasing repression will follow. Tom Hayden has written a compelling description of that process:

The people with fewest illusions about the welfare state are the poor who are served by it. When they protest, usually in the name of American ideals, an interesting reaction follows. Some among the majority react sympathetically, though not always with real understanding of the causes. But a sufficient number of opposing interests are aroused to prevent any drastic change, and often even moderate changes are blocked. The poor, who in most cases begin by politely petitioning their governors, soon take more drastic steps, thinking they can perhaps awaken the conscience of the majority or at least of higher authorities. They do awaken the consciences of some people, and to some extent they force elites to concede token changes. But at the same time, a "counterrevolution" is triggered against the potential of revolution which has been seen in the mounting protest. The system becomes deadlocked. No more than token reforms, crumbs, result for the protesters. The scale of their protest increases as they realize that appeals to conscience are inadequate. They look for methods of transcending the pressure politics that have not worked. They begin civil disobedience and disruption. The immediate reaction of the power structure is to maintain order. The police are brought into the conflict. Considerations of social, political or economic solutions to the conflict are gradually replaced by the emphasis on law and order. Violent repression becomes routine.*

* Tom Hayden, "Colonialism and Liberation," in *Politics and the Ghettos,* ed. by Roland Leslie Warren, Atherton Press, New York, 1969.

It becomes clear from the Hayden analysis—and I believe it to be accurate—that the only escape from this trap is revolution, either violent on both sides of the fence or a revolution in thinking, psychology, and political position on at least one side.

It is that second revolution that is bursting upon us today. It springs first of all from the black community. It is a revolution among black Americans in thinking about ourselves, a revolution turning upside down the analysis that had made us, the victims, describe ourselves as the cause of our own condition. It is found most concretely in the growing desire among black people to reject the kind of tribalization of color, class, and geography that has *divided* us for so long, and to bring us together as a nation within this nation.

It is found in the rejection by black people of white standards of beauty and of white-biased qualifications that have plagued us for so long.

But that alone will not do the job. We may, as we are slowly about to do, take over the major cities of this country and hold them as enclaves against increasing repression, and charge admission fees to suburban whites who must come to the city for jobs and income, and who must depend on the city as a source of police protection and utility service.

But we would also like to ask white America for simple decency of treatment, though this is a hope that many would call extremely naïve. We would like, for example, to be treated as well as American farmers are. First they were given free lands. Then they were given low-interest loans to enable them to buy farm machinery. Then the U.S. Department of Agriculture sent farm agents out to show them how to use their machines and rotate their crops. Now we pay some of them not to do anything, a form of millionaire welfarism that is scorned for poor people.

Suppose that an ADC [aid for dependent children] mother was paid not to produce at the same rate that the gentleman farmer-senator James O. Eastland is. That would mean that welfare mothers in Detroit or Chicago or Los Angeles could collect as much as $125,000 a year for not having babies.

But the revolution demands that we be allowed not more than *simply the same as other groups*. Why, we ask, must patronage be abolished as a political reward as blacks take over the cities, after political machines and favoritism have done so much for Italians and Irishmen? Why must good government advocate metropolitan-ism as a panacea to urban ills just when we are about to take over some cities? Why must some women—most of them white—and some homosexuals—most of them white—and some other groups insist that our liberation is dependent upon theirs?

The answer must be that no one—unless it is the American Indian—has priority over the justifiable demands of black people. And that only black people can set the pace, techniques, and methods used by black people in our struggle.

Foremost among these must be political action, but not the old style of machine politics of the unequal black-labor-liberal coali-tion that we have entered into like a willing bridegroom so many times in the past, only to emerge ravished and our innocence lost. Our politics must be an aggressive independent politics, free from any alliances of party or partisanship that has made us slaves first to the party of Lincoln and now to the party of Roosevelt.

We must begin to seize power where we are, in the cities and the black-belt counties of the states of the Old Confederacy. As whites flee these areas for the comfort and security of the suburbs, they create a political vacuum that we can fill. But the cities are crum-bling beneath us, and the presence of a black mayor alone will not insure that these decaying compounds will be livable again.

The black inhabitants of rural America have a better chance at achieving a decent life, for the cost of living is lower there and the people know better how to live, but even they will discover that political gains can be destroyed by an economy that still remains in the hands of the plantation bosses.

So, as we get our politics together, we must try to get our economics together as well. This means that while we reject the obviously absurd Nixonian notion of black capitalism, we must not hesitate to accept any economic advantage that might accrue to our group as a whole.

This means striving for economic plans as different as the designs for land ownership plotted by the Honorable Elijah Muhammad in the South to the neighborhood cooperatives springing up in ghettos across the country to the transfer of Mom-and-Pop stores from white hands to black ones, as well as any other plan or scheme that will put money into the pockets of black people.

This means that we cannot afford the luxury available to so many dilettantes who seek to define for us what is right and what is wrong—indeed, even what is black—in our struggle. At a time when our community seems about to draw together an alliance of cultural nationalists and political activists, of poverty workers and poverty livers, of foot-washing Baptists and the Nation of Islam, we cannot afford a Woodstock in a nation that still tolerates Watts; we cannot demand liberation for special groups until the whole group goes free.

That suggests that the fragile, sometime security of the college campus is not the proper place from which to engage in remote criticism of people who seldom see a book from year to year; that the presence of ROTC on the campus is not nearly as earth-shaking an issue as the presence of rats in the ghetto; that debates about the relative revisionism of the late Ho Chi Minh had best be neglected until we have started our own revolution here.

We must prepare for a time of trouble. If the "no-knock" and preventive detention provisions of the criminally insane District of Columbia Crime Control Act are any indication or if the unwillingness of the House Internal Security Committee to help abolish the concentration-camp features of the McCarran Act are a signal for the future, then we had better beware and prepare for hard times ahead.

Through these hard times, we might prepare ourselves with the words of Frederick Douglass, who in 1894 was asked how the race problem of the United States might be solved.

His answer then:

Let the white people of the North and South conquer their prejudices . . . let the American people cultivate kindness and humanity . . . let them give up the idea that they can be free while making the Negro a slave. Let them give up the idea that to degrade the colored man is to elevate the white man . . .

They are not required to do much. They are only required to undo the evil they have done, in order to solve their problem . . .

Put away your race prejudice. Banish the idea that one class must rule over another. Recognize the fact that the rights of the humblest of citizens are as worthy of recognition as the rights of the highest, and your problem will be solved and—whatever may be in store for you in the future, whether prosperity or adversity, whether you have foes without or foes within, whether there shall be peace or war—based on the eternal principles of truth, justice and humanity, with no class having cause for complaint or griev-ance, your Republic will stand and flourish forever.*

Truth, Justice, and Humanity. Those same principles are in no overabundance today. Is it naïve to believe that they are important and significant and should have a place in our lives?

Reports of commissions, one after another, into the riots of 1919, of 1935, of 1943, of the Watts Rebellion, appear as a "kind of Alice in Wonderland—with the same moving picture shown over and over again, the same analysis, the same recom-mendations, and the same inaction."†

For black people, the way out of this colonial status seems clear.

First, an analysis suggests that our present social system, as organized, is both incapable of solving the problem and at the same time is *a part* of the problem and cannot be appealed to or

---

* Frederick Douglass, "The Lesson of the Hour" (pamphlet), 1894.
† Dr. Kenneth Clark's testimony to the Kerner Commission.

relied upon as an independent arbiter in conflicts of which it is a part.

Next, we must assume that most white Americans lack the will, courage and intelligence to voluntarily grant black Americans independence, and that they must be forced to do it by pressure.

We must also make other assumptions:

1. That people do not discriminate for the fun of it, but that the function of prejudice is to defend special interests (social, economic, political and psychological) and that appeals to the fair play of prejudiced people are like prayers said to the wind.

2. That colonial patterns will change, and colonialists will relinquish power if they are forced to make a clear-cut choice between continuance of the colonial relationship and another clear-cut and highly cherished value—economic gain or civil peace.

3. That conflict and struggle and confrontation are necessary for social change, and

4. That the rights and lives of real human beings are at stake, and these are in the long run neither ballotable or negotiable, that such negotiation, to be meaningful, must take place between equals acting in good faith and the issues are precisely the good faith—if not the good sense—of white Americans.*

For white Americans, the question becomes whether they can give up the benefits—economic profit, political power, social status, and psychological rewards—that are derived from the status quo.

Such a movement is beginning to appear among some white youth, motivated perhaps by a surfeit of things American and the debasement of what was thought to be good. Americans today see their cities made unlivable; they see meaningless hard work done by many for the benefit of a few; they see themselves channeled by parents, schools, and draft boards; their passions and skills cannot

---

* These four statements of assumption are adopted—and somewhat adapted—by the author, from *The Negro Mood* by Lerone Bennett, Johnson Publishing Company, Chicago, 1965.

find an outlet in present-day society. The question for their future is whether they can be counted upon to discontinue the American tradition of racial arrogance.

But for white people in general, those presently satisfied with life as it is, but yearning—with all evident sincerity—to do something to alleviate the black condition, there is a program as well, spelled out by Douglass in 1894:

Now what the real problem is, we all ought to know. It is not a Negro problem, but in every sense, a great National problem. It involves the question of whether or not after all (their) boasted civilization, (their) Declaration of Independence, (their) matchless Constitution, (their) sublime Christianity, (their) wise statesmanship, whether (they) as a people possess virtue enough to solve (their) problem.

But how can their problem be solved? Let the white people of the North and South conquer their prejudices. Let them give up the idea that to degrade the colored man is to elevate the white man. Let them cease putting new wine into old bottles, or mending old garments with new cloth. Let them cultivate kindness and humanity . . .*

* Douglass, *op. cit.*

VII-
Young, Black, and Urban

I MUST ADMIT to a certain prejudice, a bias. That is race. Most of my life has been colored by race, so much of my thinking focuses on race.

In Atlanta I represent an urban constituency, people who are poor and black and old, so one may perhaps understand why the problems of the cities seem to me significant.

Black Americans are becoming, along with much of the rest of America, an urban population. In Washington, D.C., where we can't elect the mayor, we are more than 60 per cent of the population. In Richmond, Nashville, New Orleans, Jacksonville, and Birmingham we are more than 40 per cent of the population. Atlanta, Compton (California), Baltimore, Gary, St. Louis, Newark, Detroit, and Trenton have in the last decade become cities that have majority black populations.

Some things in America over the past several years have gotten better for some few of us. We can eat where we never ate before and go to school where we never went to school before and sit in the front of buses. There are more Negroes holding elective office today in all parts of this country and more Negroes making more money now than ever before, and more of us are registered to vote.

65

But for most of us, things have not gotten better. Let me quote former President Lyndon B. Johnson:

In 1948 [said Johnson, before leaving office], the 8 per cent unemployment rate for Negro teenage boys was actually less than that of whites. By 1964, the rate for Negroes had grown to 23 per cent as against 13 per cent for whites. Between 1949 and 1959, the income of Negro men relative to white men declined in every section of the country. From 1952 to 1963, the median income of Negro families compared to white actually dropped from 57 to 53 per cent. Since 1947, the number of white families living in poverty has decreased 27 per cent, while the number of non-white families living in poverty has decreased by only 3 per cent. The infant mortality of non-whites in 1940 was 70 per cent greater than whites. In 1962, it was 90 per cent greater.

To use former President Johnson's figures, the rate of unemployment for Negroes and whites in 1930 was about the same. In 1965, the Negro rate was twice as high.

Since the typical black person is poor, he faces all of the problems of poverty. For example, although there are more than five and one-half million units of substandard housing in the United States, and although congressional declarations in 1949 insisted that every American has a right to a decent home, in the better than two decades since 1949, urban renewal, highway construction, and other forces have destroyed 100,000 more homes for low-income people than have been built.

At the end of the Second World War, the median income for white families was $3,150; for blacks, a little more than $1,600. Today the average white family has an income of more than $6,500 a year, while the black family's income is about $3,500. The white family, in other words, has gained about $3,400, while the black family has gained about $1,800. In spite of laws and courts and marches and summer urban disruptions, the white family has moved twice as far ahead of its black counterpart than it was twenty yea   ago. Low-income black people suffer four times the national incidence of heart disease, ten times the incidence of defective vision. In black urban America, 30 per cent of the people have never seen a doctor; half of the expectant mothers never have prenatal care.

Statistics and figures are boring enough, as a rule. But the figures describing the plight of black people in America paint an unrelievedly gloomy picture.

In November 1971 the National Urban League made public an updated report on the black aged in this country, taking as starting point the League's pioneering study of elderly black people first published in 1960. Dr. Robert Hill, deputy director of the League's research department, concluded that the situation for aged blacks in the United States had "not improved significantly since 1960."

Life expectancy for black men actually declined from 61.1 years to 60.1 years, in contrast to a 67.5-year life expectancy for white males between 1960 and 1968, compounding an already unhappy truth: black men have far greater difficulty getting retirement benefits than white men. Most jobs held by blacks were not covered by Social Security until recently, and with a life expectancy under sixty-five, elderly blacks tend to receive minimal or nonexistent Social Security benefits. Moreover, the League report adds, more than two-thirds of the black elderly do not benefit from Medicare because of the high cost of that insurance.

More than three-fourths of the black elderly living alone had less than a $2,000 income in 1969; a third had less than $1,000. White elderly poor had on the average almost twice as much to spend.

Poverty is not the exclusive province of America's blacks. There are poor white people as well. They, however, enjoy the dubious pleasure of knowing they are not poor simply because they are white, but rather are poor in spite of their whiteness. We must, then, assume that the racial problem in this country is one of race and class. Millions of Americans are right now looking for work they won't find as unemployment hovers near 6 per cent. And another million more, no one knows how many for sure, have given up looking and are therefore no longer even counted as "unemployed" by the Labor Department. Unemployment in the black ghetto runs between 30 and 50 per cent, as compared with about 4 to 6 per cent for America as a whole during the last decade. One recent survey showed 357,000 black men and 419,000 black women officially out of work, with another 300,000 to 400,000 of the "hidden jobless" not even counted. Unemployment among black youth between the ages of sixteen and twenty-one is six times higher than for whites in the same age group.

These are awful facts and figures. They are all the more awful because they are familiar to most literate Americans and have been for more than ten years and because most literate Americans have chosen to do nothing about them.

The typical black ghetto dweller is a young adult with better than a 50 per cent chance of dropping out of high school. He is not only unemployed, but by current standards he is unemployable. He has no salable skill. Neither of his parents went beyond the eighth grade. He entered school at six but, because of overcrowding, had to attend half-day sessions. During his six years in elementary school, he attended four different schools.

What is his history and the history of his parents? What sorts of efforts have they made to improve their condition?

Since 1917, this country has had sporadic racial violence. Interestingly, it has always occurred during periods of war: 1917 to 1919, in 1943, and from 1965 into 1968. Since 1954, there have been various sorts of methods and techniques directed at solving America's white problem. These include the sit-in demonstration and nonviolent march, the pursuit of education as a barrier breaker, the use or threat of violence as inducement to change, the challenging in the courts of segregation by law, and the thrust for power through direct political action.

Legal action brought us in 1954 a statement from the nation's highest court that segregation was illegal. Almost two decades later, there are more black children attending all-black schools north of the Mason-Dixon line than there were in 1954. And, there is evidence that in 1972 there is more segregation in the North than in the South.

Each of these victories of the '60's had little meaning for most black people and the last won, the right to vote, has yet to win bread-and-butter victories for the millions now voting for the first time.

Education as a means of improving conditions for the masses dies every day that ghetto schools continue to teach that whiteness is rightness. Education is a useless tool when education systems become so large and so impersonal as to deny either parent or student or teacher the right to participate in educational decisions.

Violence as a political technique has not had a real test in this country, and the present national mood seems to suggest too that only continued repression can follow another long, hot summer.

In the immediate past few years of the life of our imaginary ghetto dweller, the country at large has begun to change, not by any means always for the better. In 1964, his community was promised that poverty would end. By 1967, a foreign war had rendered that promise, if it was ever meant, nearly useless. Between 1961 and 1964, the country officially denounced violence and war as a means of settling disputes between persons or nations. From 1965 to the present, violence has been the official policy of the government of the United States in settling her own disputes with other nations, and that belief has seeped into the police stations and slums across the land.

In 1964, our young black slum dweller thought he might get a job, but in 1972, the only job open to him was being a soldier. War has brewed anger in the black community, and it gave birth to the belief that nonviolence was only a joke to be played on or played by the black community.

It is curious to note the similarities of the national response to problems here and abroad. First one tries a little economic aid, and urges local authorities to give the peasants a bone of reform. In Vietnam this is called pacification; at home it is the poverty program. Next, when trouble erupts, counterinsurgency is used; in Vietnam, the local militias; in America, the police. When the peasants shoot back, we bomb the hell out of them. Following this thought to a logical and local ending, we might next expect to see in America the "resettlement" of Negroes into well-policed villages. In fact, that resettlement has already begun. We do live in villages and compounds within the city, policed well when police action is aimed against us, policed poorly to contain the violent and criminal forces that operate in our lives daily.

Is not the status quo as violent as any Watts or Newark or Detroit? Is it not violent to condemn to death twice the proportion of black babies as white babies in their first year? Was it not violent to send a higher proportion of black men to white men to Vietnam every year?

There are those in America who believe that a nonviolent confrontation will force a reluctant government to turn its attention homeward and toward a real solution of the white problem in America. There are those who believe that progress of a sort is being made and will be made, and, like Scarlett O'Hara, believe tomorrow will be another—and perhaps a better—day. There are those who believe that giving some small power—the appearance of control of neighborhood schools, decision making in some forms of government—will hold off the day of Armageddon that many think is coming.

And there are those for whom the major problem has become the right to smoke pot or to throw flowers, while for others the fight is for the right to breathe clean air or to throw bombs.

Nonviolent confrontations have their place. The English gave in to Gandhi's demonstrations. We ought to remember that the English were said to have a conscience, while this government is thought to have none. Out of all of the members of the United States House of Representatives, only thirty-six could be found to support the recommendations of the President's Commission on Civil Disorders. If this is any indication of conscience, it is a sad one.

In the comparison of tactics in Vietnam with black Americans, there is one huge significant difference: The nation was willing to spend billions of dollars a year in Vietnam, while there's no comparable financial commitment in the ghettos. At one point we were spending roughly $30 billion per year to interfere with the political future of eighteen million Vietnamese. We surely ought to be able to spend that much on twenty-two million black Americans whose future affects this country much more than the lesson in democracy being taught in Southeast Asia's rice paddies.

Violence is a preoccupation with those who wonder what black America wants. They dismiss the violence of wrenching a people from their homeland, separating mother from father, parents from children; the violence of the slave plantation; the violence of the racist South; the institutional violence that produces an infant mortality rate among blacks that is twice that for whites and rising; the violence in men's minds that devised Jim Crow.

It is violent simply to be black in America today.

There are answers to our problems, but they must be sought among the troubled and among the young. One must know, if not understand, what life is like in the dark ghetto today.

"The dark ghettos," Dr. Kenneth Clark has written, "are social, political, educational . . . and above all . . . economic colonies. Their inhabitants are subject people, victims of the greed, cruelty, insensitivity, guilt and fear of their masters."

The terms "colony" and "colonized people" correctly describe the condition of those millions who even today are deserting the mechanized feudal system of the South for the more highly mechanized, and more highly segregated in a sophisticated way, ghettos of the North and West.

From the colonies must come a new movement and a new method. We ought perhaps to remind ourselves in passing of the method an earlier colony on these shores took to free itself from oppression: that method was armed rebellion, insurrection, seizure of property, death and destruction, the American way of 1776.

VIII-
City Too Busy to Hate

UNLIKE MOST American cities my home city of Atlanta is in many ways a good place to live. It was once called the city "too busy to hate" by the late Mayor William B. Hartsfield, and nationally it has had a progressive image on racial matters. Sometimes, it is clear, that progressive image is more image than progressive. But it is an interesting city, and most people like living in Atlanta.

I can remember giving Atlanta's future, political and economic, a great deal of thought in the months not long after President Nixon entered the White House. Perhaps this was natural, this turning in thought to my own city, full of the knowledge that the man elected President of the United States had little use for the black or the poor or the young. He was elected, in part, through the most callous exploitation of racist politics, certainly on a national level, in modern times. There seemed little hope or likelihood of influencing an Administration whose chief Southern adviser was the old Dixiecrat himself, Senator Strom Thurmond. And this was, unhappily, an accurate impression, as events have since demonstrated.

But back to Atlanta. One can remember in the early days of the Nixon Administration when the Department of Defense announced it was awarding $9.4 million in contracts to three Southern textile firms on the "promise" that they wouldn't discriminate anymore. I remember thinking this was a bold new approach to human relations, the Nixon technique. Perhaps, I thought, the Ku Klux Klan could now "promise" not to beat or intimidate black people, "promise" not to burn their homes. Perhaps the Atlanta Board of Education could "promise" to give decent-quality integrated education to all of the children of the city. Perhaps the owners of slum housing in Atlanta could be persuaded to "promise" not to rent dilapidated houses to poor people in the future.

If these thoughts were not enough, I can recall that in that same period, early in the Nixon Administration, the former Vice-President of the United States, the former Presidential candidate of his party, came to Atlanta to attend a funeral.

Mixing a little business with a solemn occasion, he met with local Democrats, telling them he wanted a united Democratic Party. But who was invited to such a meeting? Not those who had fought for an open, integrated, *democratic* Democratic Party in Georgia. Not those who had demanded that the inner workings of the majority party in my home state be opened to all of the people, but rather among those present were those who stood for the status quo, who argued that they would do better in the future; in short, those there were the stalwarts of the hand-picked Lester Maddox delegation to the 1968 Democratic national convention.

In fact, if my memory serves, the Negro members of the hand-picked group who so loyally stood with the Democratic Party throughout that election were not even invited.

So, the early part of 1969 was not a time to hold out much hope for black people in America, in Atlanta or anywhere else. Yet, for those of us in the city of Atlanta, the city too busy to hate, it seemed surely there must be hope for us. Surely, we thought, this city is better than the rest of the U.S.A., and surely here we have some chance of improving our condition.

In 1969, the city of Atlanta was about to face a critical election, a crisis if you will, another of the crises that the city has faced, and overcome, since the days when, as the old song says, "Sherman marched along/ To the sea,/ Like Moses riding/ On a Bumblebee."

Most of these crises, like that first one, had to do in some way with race. There was the terrible Atlanta riot, just after the turn of the century, when white men ran like rabid dogs through black Atlanta, raping, burning, looting, and killing as they ran.

Most recently, however, Atlanta crises have been handled with greater dispatch. When the public schools were integrated here, by order of a federal court, because the city was "too busy to hate" and therefore also too busy to bother about obeying the law of the land, former Mayor Hartsfield managed to turn the occasion into a Chamber of Commerce tour of the city's virtues. Lunch-counter integration was handled with the same flair for public relations. The occasional racial flare-ups that have occurred since then have shown that this city's fathers are not losing their expertise in explaining away Atlanta's racial divisions. The Atlanta Board of Education, until the most recent election, adopted these same public-relations techniques in a vain attempt to explain away years of neglect and callousness in dealing with the black community.

With each increasing and escalating demand from the black community, the response from white Atlanta has been less moderate, more condescending, and more appreciative of the rapidly increasing black population in Atlanta.

That population is largely poor. It is poorly educated, both because it is composed of migrants from rural Georgia and because it is the product of a racially segregated school system presided over until recently by a board whose loyalties lay in financial Atlanta, and not in improving the minds of young black men and women.

Atlanta's city election of 1969 was significant in a variety of ways. It served as prelude, for one thing, for what will likely happen in the next city election in 1973. But the 1969 election was significant for another reason. Black Atlanta, mostly the poor and poorly educated section of Atlanta, along with the minority of black Atlanta living with some affluence and leisure, nearly 48 per cent of the total population at the time by most estimates, found itself nearly in a position to take control of the reins of city government.

The take-over did not occur in 1969. It was, frankly, not likely to occur that year. The possibility of electing a black mayor in Atlanta was slim, largely because of the first law of racial politics: that most white people will not, if given a choice, vote for a black man, however qualified he may be. So, while the 1969 election was not likely to be one that would see the last battle of Atlanta fought, it was likely to be the last one in which the grand coalition of all black people and some few of the white people decided who would sit in the mayor's chair.

That old coalition has been a strong one. It put the fear of God into William B. Hartsfield and re-elected him more than any other American mayor. It elected his successor, former Mayor Ivan Allen, and re-elected him to a second term, and would have elected him again if he had chosen to run again.

But despite its effectiveness in providing moderate government in Atlanta, the coalition was unwieldy and basically unfair. It was unwieldy because it allowed a minority of the white voters in Atlanta to dictate to all of the black voters, a subtle kind of racial "whitemail" that worked for more than twenty-five years. Under this kind of "whitemail," the specter of a Lester Maddox as possible mayor was always raised before the black community and the black community always responded in fear with votes for a moderate on election day.

But the black part of the old Atlanta coalition had little or nothing to do with selecting candidates, choosing issues, or influencing any other election except that for the top job, the mayor's office. Under Atlanta's weak mayor system, having a moderate or liberal white or black mayor means little or nothing to most of black Atlanta.

So, in 1969, it was likely that the old pattern would be repeated;

two or more white liberal candidates would spar for the promise of support from the banks and the business community, the black community would threaten to run a candidate of its own, but in the end, all of black Atlanta and a small part of white Atlanta would elect a white mayor who would be the last of his race to govern this city.

The 1969 election, in fact, worked out that way, though in a somewhat unexpected fashion.

The campaign should have been an occasion for sober discussion of the political and economic future of Atlanta. But the campaign rhetoric turned out to be as disappointing as campaign rhetoric frequently is. That race for mayor was about as exciting as shooting fish in a barrel.

Two of the four main candidates decided that the main issue was law and order. One seemed to mean this as did George Wallace, indicating that should you lie down in front of his car he would run over you; the other, a Republican, adopted the slogan, as did the leader of his political party, to mean that if you should lie down in front of his car, he'd order his chauffeur to run over you. Some candidates talked about traffic and education and taxes and other such issues that are important ones to many voters. But in the city's black community, in Atlanta and in other cities, the only important issue for us must be: Which of these candidates is going to do something for us?

That means, which one is going to see that public housing is dispersed throughout the city? Which one is going to see that black policemen and firemen in the city are no longer *Jim Crowed?* Which one is going to integrate city hall, with all of its jobs? Which one is going to keep Hunter Street and Auburn Avenue in the black community as clean as upper Peachtree Stree? Which one is going to stop the systematic destruction of black residential neighborhoods by halting the spread of commercial development and jerry-built apartments? Which one is going to revitalize urban renewal so it does not continue to mean "Negro removal"? Which one is going to give us the facts, and not merely the substitutes and subterfuges that black people in Atlanta have become so accustomed to?

These questions and questions like them could apply to almost any mayor's race in any American city.

Or, as a few years ago, as it was put by a black disc jockey running for a position on the Board of Aldermen, Atlanta's black people had received for their votes through the years only "street lights on Auburn Avenue and black policemen who can't arrest anybody but you."

It is a sad but true fact that for most black people, Atlanta has been more dream than reality. The tragedy of a city election like that of Atlanta in 1969 was that the mayor's race, uninspiring as it was, tended to take valuable attention away from often more important races for aldermen and the school board.

Surely Atlanta's Board of Education in the 1950's and 1960's was comprised, with one or two exceptions, of the sorriest bunch of public officials in the city. They were and still are largely businessmen who seem to think that children and the massive problems of school faculty and pupil integration can be placed on balance sheets and added up at a profit at the end of the year.

Individual elections for aldermanic seats are so important in Atlanta and in most cities because, peopled by the right people, the Board of Aldermen is the body that can make important decisions about the lives of the poor and the black, groups that have come increasingly to dominate urban areas. They can order department heads to integrate their staffs; they can control deployment of policemen so that my constituents, for example, do not have to complain to me about a lack of law and order in my constituency; they can insure that Atlanta's next public-housing project gets erected in Buckhead, or some other white suburban section, rather than being crammed once more into the crowded section of the inner city, where all of Atlanta's public-housing projects have always been crammed.

But, again, those important races for aldermen and the Board of Education tended in the 1969 Atlanta election to be over-shadowed by interest in the question of whether a black man could be elected mayor of this city. The same question is likely to over-shadow such vital races again in 1973.

The history of the two other similar efforts shows a situation markedly different from Atlanta in 1969 (though not so different from what Atlanta is likely to be in 1973). In Cleveland and in Gary, the black voting population on election day was a good deal closer to 50 per cent than in Atlanta. In Cleveland and in Gary, Carl Stokes and Richard Hatcher each won initially with no more than a 2,000-vote margin, Stokes winning only in his second attempt. Hatcher could, in fact, have won without a single white vote.

Of course, Atlanta is not Cleveland or Gary. Atlanta is the city too busy to hate. And Atlanta in its 1969 election was faced with having to decide on election day what it wanted for itself, what it wanted for its people, and what kind of person it wants to do these things for them. That election in 1969, as it turned out, was curiously indecisive. And, for the most part, the white voters of Atlanta voted their race just as they had for the most part in Gary and Cleveland.

The Atlanta mayor's race was especially frustrating for black voters. A qualified black candidate ran, Dr. Horace Tate, an edu-cator and member of the Board of Education. It seems quite pos-sible, in retrospect, that Tate could have been elected if he had received solid backing in the black community. Some black com-munity leaders, however, chose to support a white candidate in-stead, their argument to black voters being that a black candidate had no chance of winning, some among them feeling too the weight of a private unstated argument: they did not want any *other* black man to become the first black mayor of Atlanta.

The upshot of this was that Dr. Tate polled a majority of the votes in the black community but fell short of a spot in the two-man runoff, running a close third.

Then-Vice-Mayor Sam Massell, the white candidate who had

received more black votes than any other, led the field. He was in a runoff with businessman Rodney Cook, a Republican. I spoke earlier of the long-time coalition between some white voters and all black voters that for years had elected Atlanta mayors. That coalition survived, in a sense, in 1969 but in a quite altered fashion. The white downtown bankers and businessmen who had dominated that coalition supported Cook, the loser. Massell won the runoff election with almost solid black voter support.

Mayor Massell has since that election, in some ironic ways, moved with the times. Speaking to The Hungry Club, whose membership is made up primarily of professional black people, the mayor urged them to "think white," which has the ring a bit of saying to Israeli Premier Golda Meir "think Arab." In late 1971, Massell unveiled a plan to have the legislature merge Atlanta with the predominanty white suburbs just north of the city. There was nothing racial in the plan, insisted the mayor, though its only immediate concrete result seemed to be to boost the percentage of white voters in the city while reducing the number of black voters. Some people believed that Mayor Massell, who ran as the *de facto* "black man's" candidate in 1969, aimed to put himself in the position to run as the "white man's" candidate in 1973.

But regardless of who becomes mayor of Atlanta, life will go on. It will presumably get better for some people, although it is clearly getting worse for black Americans, especially those in cities.

We live in an increasingly hostile world that assumes that because we now can eat at Rich's, Atlanta's best-known department store, and sit downstairs at the Fox Theater that our lives are magically transformed.

We are at present being governed by a hostile national Administration, the bland leading the bland. Shortly after Reconstruction, when federal troops were employed across the South, and black and white men had an opportunity to govern this section of the country, an American President made a dastardly deal with the Bourbons of the Old South. For ten years before then, black and white school children went to school together, black men helped govern all of the states of the Old Confederacy, black men set up the South's first free public school system, abolished imprisonment for debt, and established free male suffrage. But a ruthless and ambitious politician sold the trusting black people of the South back to the Bourbons, the troops were recalled, and Jim Crow reared his ugly head. The same process was repeated in Miami Beach in 1968. Its echoes, the taint of shoddy bargains kept, will be in the convention hall with the Republicans in San Diego in the summer of 1972.

The other major political party has moved on the national level to reform itself, in many ways, if not completely and not always forthrightly. Yet on the local level, it often remains in the grip of a small group of men, elected by no one, serving only their own interests.

That situation may not be dealt with in Atlanta, but it is being dealt with in other parts of the South. In Greene County, Alabama, black men now control the County Commission and the Board of Education. In Hancock County, Georgia, black men hold majority power. And in southwest Georgia, black men and women are preparing to grab the reins of government and build a real democracy in Maddox country.

That situation will be dealt with in Atlanta as well, again without regard to who governs the city or whether the city continues to exist or not, at least in its present form. Black Atlanta may never achieve political primacy, but it can do a great deal to insure that its future is brighter and healthier than its past.

We can do that by insisting that any white man doing business in our community must have a black person as full partner by, say, the end of 1972, or he must stop doing business at all. We can follow the lead of black people in Chicago and Pittsburgh, and insist that when new construction is begun in our neighborhoods, if black people don't work, no one works.

We can begin to insist that the schools in our neighborhoods, even under the control of a city-wide Board of Education, share some measure of that control with the people of those neighborhoods.

We can, in fact, begin to exert real control over that little bit of Atlanta that is ours by virtue of our squatters' rights. We can— and I believe we will—adopt the slogan that insists that if an institution operates in our community, then we must control it. We can no longer afford to believe that the white man's ice is colder, his sugar sweeter, or his medicine better.

About one hundred years ago, my state of Georgia had one black congressman and thirty-two black men in the state legislature. The legislature expelled all those thirty-two but one, who was fair-skinned and therefore by their reasoning neither black nor white.

One of those legislators, Henry M. Turner, the gentleman from Bibb County, rose before he was expelled and delivered a speech that ought still to have some meaning for white Georgians—and white Americans—today. He said then:

The great question, sirs, is this, am I a man? If I am, I claim the rights of such. . . .

Why sir, though we are not white, we have accomplished much. . . . And what do we ask in return? Do we ask for compensation for the sweat our fathers bore for you—for the tears you have caused, and for the hearts you have broken, the lives you have curtailed, and the blood you have spilled? Do we ask retaliation? We ask it not. We are willing to let the dead past bury its dead, but we ask you now for our rights. You have all the elements of superiority on your side; you have our money and your own; you have our education and your own; you have your land and our own. . . . It is extraordinary that a race such as yours, professing gallantry, and chivalry, and education, and superiority, living in a land where Bibles are read and gospel truths are spoken, and where courts of justice are presumed to exist. It is extraordinary to say that with all these advantages on your side, you can still make war on the defenseless black man. You may expel us, gentlemen, but I believe you will repent it. The black man cannot protect a country if the country doesn't protect him, and if tomorrow, a war should arise, I would not raise a musket to defend a country where my manhood is denied. The fashionable way in Georgia when hard work is to be done is for the white man to sit at ease, while the black man does all the work, but sir, I will say this much to the colored men of Georgia: never lift your finger in defense of Georgia, unless Georgia acknowledges that you are men, and invests you with all the rights pertaining to manhood.

That last sentiment could hold true for most black Americans. Even while Mayor Massell has served in office since the 1969 election, important political changes have been taking place. The first important continuing change is that black Atlanta has become a population—but not voting—majority of the city. Attempts to dilute this black majority will be made through legislative action, court action, petition, and every other possible method known to man.

Making deals with black legislators has largely failed, and in each instance, the slightly unholy alliance of the good people of Sandy Springs, in white suburbia north of Atlanta, and the black legislators of the inner city has served to beat back every attempt to dilute the growing black strength of inner-city Atlanta. The white suburban dwellers believe, apparently, that they can take advantage of all the city's benefits and avoid all its problems by remaining outside the city limits; the black legislators oppose what often seem cynical efforts to undermine them politically. Expansion, with guarantees of black political parity, is not always objectionable. Expansion with a concurrent dilution of black political power must always be opposed. Now, proper arrangements for the widening of the city limits might be made if there were guarantees that such an expanded government would include proper opportunity for fair representation of this city's black voters. They have not had that guarantee in most proposals.

Those who predict that a black Atlanta will mean an eroding tax base, less money for city services, or even more segregated schools somehow are missing the point. Every American city, white or black, is losing its tax base. Chicago and New York have proportionately less of a black population than Atlanta, but they face the same sorts of problems, and the schools of Chicago are probably more segregated than those of Atlanta, if that is possible.

But consider the city of Atlanta. Its banks and schools, its businesses and sports, are not going to pick up and leave. The Atlanta Braves and Hawks and Falcons are not going to leave because the customers become blacker and blacker each year. The new Equitable Building on Forsyth Street or John Portman's Peachtree Center complex are not going to be torn down and moved to an outlying county because the people who walk by are blacker in 1972 than they were in 1968 or in 1970. The capital of the state of Georgia will still be in Atlanta. Business and commerce will continue to be the lifeblood of this city, this center of the Southeast.

Yet Atlanta will likely exist in a state of political cold war between the races over the next several years. White Atlanta will begin to get more and more restless, will continue to challenge the ability, qualifications, or even the correctness of a black-dominated government in Atlanta. The stage will be set either for an orderly transition of the reins of government, like that which took place temporarily in Cleveland and permanently in Gary, or for the kind of white selfishness and black impotence characteristic of municipal government in our nation's capital or in ghost cities like Newark, New Jersey.

In both Newark and Washington, a black majority, sullen, angry, politically helpless despite their numbers, is ruled by absentee landlords—in one instance an ethnic political machine, in the other the worst racists in Congress. But Newark's blacks have begun to overcome.

Atlanta's future can parallel either one of these. This city could see black people become a political majority while white Atlanta retains control. That kind of control, despite an overwhelming black population, can be maintained by having white-selected candidates represent black Atlanta in city hall and on the Board of Aldermen or by divisiveness and powerlessness in the black community that will castrate it politically.

This is the kind of divisiveness that occurs when two or more organizations try to register the same voters, when two or more organizations with almost the same name—one with a grass-roots membership and the other with nearly none—compete for the same following. It is the kind of powerlessness that results when voting turnouts in black communities are less than 65 per cent. It is the kind of powerlessness that is readily seen by a glance at black membership on appointed boards in Atlanta and Fulton County. It would appear from a look at that list that all Negroes in Atlanta have only four family names.

This kind of indirect white domination can occur when shadow candidates appear, financed from outside the black community, hand-picked by forces that want only to exploit the potential of the black vote. There are already formed in Atlanta well-meaning groups of affluent whites who want to discover and finance black candidates who will be acceptable to the city's white people.

But perhaps, despite every prediction of gloom, Atlanta can see the old slogans of the early civil rights movement live again. Black and white together, we shall overcome, and all the rest of what many thought was a forgotten dream, already deferred.

Its future depends on the willingness of the black community to mold itself into a solid, cohesive group, a strong political unit where ties of personality, party, and organization can be submerged for the greater good.

It will depend on the willingness of white Atlanta to accept the inevitable future, the fact that this will be a black city, and that black people are, like white people, capable of rule or ruin. It will depend on a marked decrease of the kind of sophisticated racism that pervades this city. That kind of racism makes those who know better, both black and white, predict that a black government means an end to civilization. It makes those who know better refuse to support the legitimate demands of the black community for integrated quality education in this city or for democratic reform of this city's method of selecting public officials. It is the kind of racism that means that any black candidate, however gifted, qualified, respected, and able, cannot be elected mayor of this city until black people constitute 51 per cent or more of the *voting* population.

If that kind of evil can be defeated, if the splintered, scattered forces in the black community can be pulled together, if honest, open, democratic, and fair coalitions can be made with black and white people here, then this city and others like it have a chance.

Atlanta could build the kind of city that could take as its motto the words of the late Dr. W. E. B. Du Bois, who wrote while he was a teacher at Atlanta University:

. . . I believe in liberty for all men: the space to stretch their arms and their souls, the right to breathe and the right to vote: the freedom to choose their friends, and enjoy the sunshine and ride on the railroads, uncursed by color: thinking, dreaming, working as they will in a kingdom of God and love. Finally, I believe in patience: patience with the weakness of the weak and the strength of the strong, the prejudice of the ignorant and the ignorance of the blind, patience with the tardy triumph of joy and the chastening of sorrow: patience with God.*

* W. E. B. Du Bois, in Darkwater, *Voices from Within the Veil*. Harcourt, Brace & Howe, New York, 1920.

IX-

The Panthers and Bobby Seale, Angela Davis, and George Jackson

ONE of the sorry aftermaths of the 1968 Democratic convention was the conspiracy trial of Bobby Seale and seven other defendants for allegedly planning and creating the demonstrations and disturbances in Chicago during the convention.

It is a source of continuing amazement to discover people who have eyes and yet will not see. Or the people who, perhaps because of some psychological need, insist on seeing sinister plots behind every rosebush. It's an old story to Southerners who were active in the civil rights movement in the 1960's, when almost any Deep South sheriff believed he had faced up to the often simple and heartfelt demands for racial justice by dismissing such sentiments as the creations of "outside agitators" who were no doubt getting their orders directly from Moscow.

It has become more common on the national scene in the last several years also to dismiss anything uncomfortable, things like civil rights and peace demonstrations ana rent strikes, as the results of plots and conspiracies.

Take the Chicago Democratic convention in 1968. Given the mood of the country, the crescendo of virtual rebellion against the useless carnage of the war in Vietnam, the growing conviction that the government of the United States had lied repeatedly to the American people about that war, the national unease about other domestic issues, from civil rights to the plight of the cities, given these things, there is little wonder that there were demonstrations in the streets. The head-knocking brutal tactics of Chicago police were, conceivably, even predictable, but they certainly added violence to an already tense and simmering situation.

To suggest that any eight people could plot or create that situation is a somewhat simple-minded view. One might as well suggest these same eight incredibly powerful people planned the escalation of the Vietnam war, the opposition to that war, and the political climate that propelled Senator Eugene McCarthy in a matter of months from a relatively little known senator to a major national figure because he had the guts to speak out against an Administration of his own political party, when few other men of influence had that kind of courage.

Yet, again, there are many people who cling to the simple-minded view. It is no doubt easier, more comfortable.

I found one of the most fascinating examples of this kind of theorizing in the January 3, 1972, issue of *Barron's,* published by Dow Jones & Company, Inc. *Barron's* is the Bible of the American business community.

Barron's is considered a highly accurate, informative business and financial weekly. But to say that it is politically and socially conservative is an understatement. For example, *Barron's* recently ran a major article about child labor. Its thrust? That the child-labor conditions of a century and more ago really weren't too bad; that child labor was probably on the whole good for the economy and the children, even though those youngsters sometimes worked sixteen hours a day, often in dim light that cost them their vision.

The January 1972 article in *Barron's* was called "America the Radical" and described a group called the Socialist Scholars Conference, which was founded in 1964 and was dissolved in 1970.

It was started by six Marxist historians, according to the article, who set out to achieve the "radicalization" of America. This wondrous group was, again according to the article, responsible for planning the demonstrations against the Vietnam war, the racial conflicts in many cities, the violence at the 1968 Democratic convention, student uprisings, and, further, "for activities of 'the Movement,' that amorphous revolutionary grouping with connections reaching round the world, from Vietcong to kidnaping Tupamaros, from Parisian cobblestone-hurling anarchists to Mexican student-cadre snipers."

If the authorities in Chicago had only known! Then they could have put on trial these Marxist historians, rather than Bobby Seale and his codefendants.

The quality of logic and reasoning in the article can be perhaps indicated by another quotation: "Not only did the Socialist Scholars' activist allies at home help the Vietcong from inside this country . . . but also their foreign allies, such as Belgian Marxist Ernest Mandel, did everything possible to bring about the kind of activist situation that eventually resulted in the killings at Kent State University in Ohio."

Murder was done at Kent State when National Guardsmen shot down four students. The Ohio grand jury that exonerated those guardsmen in favor of indicting college students would no doubt have read the *Barron's* article with interest. They might have moved to indict Ernest Mandel too.

But let us consider the cause of Bobby Seale in the aftermath of the Chicago 1968 Democratic convention.

One cannot read the transcript of that "trial" without concluding that what Bobby Seale and the other members of the Chicago 8 had really done was to upset someone, somewhere, who was determined to "get" them in revenge.

And Bobby Seale was "got." Judge Julius J. Hoffman sentenced him to four years in jail for contempt of court, this though he was never convicted of the conspiracy charges that brought about the trial in the first place. Nor of charges of complicity in the murder of Alex Rackley, a former member of the Black Panther Party, in Connecticut. In fact, those conspiracy and murder accusation charges eventually came to nothing. Seale spent time enough in jail, though not that four years for contempt. But the concern here ought to be for the way his trial in Chicago was handled. It is important in understanding why many black Americans fear our system of justice.

Bobby Seale, thirty-three, a former law student, succeeded Huey P. Newton, another former law student, as chairman of the Oakland, California-based Black Panther Party.

It was Newton's familiarity with California law that encouraged the Panthers to carry weapons openly in Oakland when they began policing the police. One can read in the transcript Seale's insistence that he be dealt with according to law, that he be allowed to choose his own lawyer or, lacking that, be allowed to defend himself. That is the surface conflict that caused him to be bound and gagged, and eventually sentenced to four years in jail.

It is not likely that many readers of this book will have either attended the Bobby Seale trial, as I did as a witness, or will have since that time read the transcript.

For this reason, I want to quote, very briefly, from what was a long and laborious judicial proceeding. It is necessary, really, in order to have some feeling of the flavor of that courtroom scene. The basis for most of the sixteen separate charges of contempt of court against Seale was whether attorney William Kunstler was in fact Seale's lawyer. Both Seale and Kunstler denied it. But Kunstler was one of several lawyers listed as counsel for all the defendants before the trial actually got under way. Another of the attorneys, the one Seale said was his lawyer specifically, fell ill at the time of the trial. Seale then asked to be permitted to act as his own lawyer. Judge Julius Hoffman refused his request and ruled that Kunstler was officially Seale's attorney, no matter what Kunstler or Seale said.

The following exchange took place in the morning session on October 14, 1969, as Seale interrupted one of the defense lawyers.

SEALE: Hey, you don't speak for me. I would like to speak on behalf of my own self and have my counsel handle my case in behalf of myself.

How come I can't speak in behalf of myself? I am my own legal counsel. I don't want these lawyers to represent me.

JUDGE HOFFMAN: You have a lawyer of record and he has been of record here since the 24th.

SEALE: I have been arguing that before that jury heard one shred of evidence. I don't want these lawyers because I can take my own legal defense and my lawyer is Charles Garry.

JUDGE HOFFMAN: I direct you, sir, to remain quiet.

SEALE: And just be railroaded?

JUDGE HOFFMAN: Will you remain quiet?

SEALE: I want to defend myself, do you mind, please?

JUDGE HOFFMAN: Let the record show that the defendant Seale continued to speak after the court courteously requested him to remain quiet.

This exchange was cited as one of the sixteen grounds for contempt. Penalty: three months in jail.

Another exchange took place on October 22 during argument on a motion by attorney Kunstler for permission to withdraw as counsel for Seale.

SEALE: Can I speak on that and answer his argument?

JUDGE HOFFMAN: No. This is not your motion, sir. Your motion has been decided.

SEALE: In other words, I can't speak in behalf of myself?

JUDGE HOFFMAN: Not at this time, sir.

SEALE: Why not?

JUDGE HOFFMAN: Because this is your lawyer's motion.

SEALE: That ain't my lawyer.

JUDGE HOFFMAN: This is not your motion. This is the motion of Mr. William Kunstler for leave to withdraw as your lawyer.

SEALE: Well, this man has misconstrued a whole lot of things concerning my right to defend myself and he knows he did. They can jack you up and get you to sit up there and say rotten, crazy stuff concerning my right to defend myself.

JUDGE HOFFMAN: I would request the marshal to ask the young man to sit down.

SEALE: Well, I want my right to defend myself and this man knew, I indicated to him he was not my counsel at the very beginning when I first got here and arrived here and was in jail.

JUDGE HOFFMAN: That motion—since you will not listen to the Court, you may sit down. Have him sit down, Mr. Marshal.

SEALE: I still want my right to defend myself. A railroad operation, and you know it, from Nixon on down. They got you running around here violating my constitutional rights.

End of exchange. A separate contempt charge. Penalty: another three months.

Let one final example suffice. The following occurred during the morning session of October 29, after the cross-examination of a witness had been completed.

JUDGE HOFFMAN: Is there any redirect examination?

SEALE: Before the redirect, I would like to request again—demand—that I be able to cross-examine the witness. My lawyer is not here. I think I have a right to defend myself in this courtroom.

JUDGE HOFFMAN: Take the jury out, and they may go to lunch with the usual order.

SEALE: You have George Washington and Benjamin Franklin sitting in a picture behind you, and they was slave owners. That's what they were. They owned slaves. You are acting in the same manner, denying me my constitutional rights being able to cross-examine this witness.

(The following continuation of the proceedings occurred in open court, but out of the presence and hearing of the jury.)

SEALE: You have had direct examination, we have cross-examination by the other defendants' lawyers, and I have a right to cross-examine the witness.

JUDGE HOFFMAN: Mr. Seale, I have admonished you previously—

SEALE: I have a right to cross-examine the witness.

JUDGE HOFFMAN: —what might happen to you if you keep on talking.

SEALE: I still have the right to cross-examine the witness. Why don't you recognize my constitutional rights?

JUDGE HOFFMAN: Mr. Kunstler has his appearance on record as your attorney.

SEALE: He is not. He is not. He is not my lawyer, and you know that.

JUDGE HOFFMAN: He is, I don't know . . .

SEALE: You know that.

JUDGE HOFFMAN: I know that he is, and I know this is just an entire device here . . .

SEALE: He is not my lawyer. You have forced—you have made your choice of who you think should represent me. That is not true. I make the choice of Charles R. Garry to represent me.

JUDGE HOFFMAN: We are going to recess now, young man. If you keep this up . . .

SEALE: Look, old man, if you keep up denying me my constitutional rights, you are being exposed to the public and the world that you do not care about people's constitutional rights to defend themselves.

JUDGE HOFFMAN: I will tell you that what I indicated yesterday might happen to you . . .

SEALE: Happen to me? What can happen to me more than what Benjamin Franklin and George Washington did to black people in slavery? What can happen to me more than that?

JUDGE HOFFMAN: And I might add since it has been said here

that all of the defendants support you in your position that I might conclude that they are bad risks for bail, and I say that to you, Mr. Kunstler, that if you can't control your client . . .

SEALE: I still demand my constitutional rights as a defendant in this case to defend myself. I demand the right to be able to cross-examine the witness. He has made statements against me and I want my right to . . . I want the constitutional right to defend myself. I want the right to cross-examine the witness, and why don't you recognize the law of this land and give me my constitutional right to defend myself?

That ends the last part of the transcript that I'll quote. It was the same afternoon following the last exchange that Judge Hoffman ordered Bobby Seale shackled to a chair and gagged while the court proceedings went on.

I've quoted only three of sixteen exchanges, each of which was cited separately as a contempt charge. Each drew a three-month penalty, the penalties to be served consecutively, for a total of a four-year sentence. The exchanges have a depressing sameness about them. Charles Rembar, lawyer and author, wrote what might be described as a free translation of the testimony, summing up these exchanges.

DEFENDANT: I want a lawyer.
JUDGE: You've got a lawyer.
DEFENDANT: He's not my lawyer.
ATTORNEY: I'm not his lawyer.
JUDGE: You are his lawyer.
ATTORNEY: I resigned.
JUDGE: You can't resign.
ATTORNEY: He fired me.
JUDGE: He can't do that.
DEFENDANT: *I did* do that.
JUDGE: Let's get on, and don't make trouble.

DEFENDANT: There's just one lawyer that I want; no sub will do.

JUDGE: This man here is highly competent.

ATTORNEY: Thanks a lot.

JUDGE: Shut up, sir.

DEFENDANT: If I cannot have the lawyer of my choice, I'll be my own.

JUDGE: Not that either.

DEFENDANT: Let me cross-examine.

JUDGE: You may not cross-examine.

DEFENDANT: You're a racist.

JUDGE: You're misbehaving.

DEFENDANT: I am not.

JUDGE: You sure are, sir.

DEFENDANT: I just insist upon the Constitution.

JUDGE: You're not fit to mention that.

DEFENDANT: I just claim the Bill of Rights—like jury trial, like free speech, like due process, habeas corpus, right to bail.

JUDGE: The hell you do. You're in contempt, sir. Go to jail.*

The clash between Judge Hoffman, and what he represents, and Bobby Seale, and what he represents, was a far more significant matter than it might easily appear.

The Chicago 8 were a test of the 1968 Conspiracy Act, passed as a rider attached by South Carolina Senator Strom Thurmond to the Civil Rights Act. The Act makes it a crime, in effect, to travel from Baltimore to Newark to speak if and when your speech is likely to incite someone to riot. The someone may be a listener who agrees with your words or a listener who becomes outraged and violent because he disagrees with them. Therefore if a TVA employee had been angered by Barry Goldwater's assertion that TVA should be sold or if a St. Petersburg pensioner had become enraged at Goldwater's plea to lower Social Security, and had

* *The "Trial" of Bobby Seale.* Arbor House Publishing Co., New York, 1970.

engaged in either violence or riotous behavior, Senator Goldwater might have become a defendant in a trial like the one we have witnessed in Chicago. Fortunately for him, it was not law when he spoke.

It was known in Congress as the "Rap Brown amendment" and would never have applied to the Goldwaters of the world anyway. It was designed for the Rap Browns and the Stokely Carmichaels and the Bobby Seales. It was designed to punish those whose words might inflame mobs in Chicago's streets or blacks in Newark's alleys, not to punish inflammatory Presidents and mayors and senators and leaders of political parties.

That is what Bobby Seale and the Chicago 8 did. Of all the eight, Seale was in Chicago for the shortest amount of time during convention week, less than forty-eight hours. He did not know all of his so-called coconspirators, nor did all of them know one another. He made only one speech while he was in Chicago.

But he came to the Democratic convention—as he came into Judge Hoffman's courtroom—representing the largest, most disciplined, organized group of radical blacks in the country. He came as a leader of an organization with a history of no-nonsense aggressiveness, of a willingness to stand up against policemen, an organization with a history of social service to the black community and an organization whose stated purpose is the revolutionary overthrow of oppression and wrong in the United States.

At the trial, he came before Judge Julius Hoffman, seventy-four-year-old former law partner of Chicago's Mayor Richard Daley, a man known as a "hanging judge" to defense lawyers in the city.

The two men, one eating lunch in the Standard Club every noon, the other led from the courtroom to a cell, met in a paneled room on the twenty-fifth floor of Chicago's United States Courthouse.

How different their lives must have been until the moment they met in court. How different they have been since their meeting. Seale left the courtroom with no judicial determination of his guilt as a conspirator, facing a four-year jail term and facing further clashes with other judges. Judge Hoffman left, secure in his own mind that justice had been done, after sentencing other defendants to long terms for contempt.

But the Panthers, and the departure they represent, will continue beyond Seale and Hoffman. The Panthers represent the latest turn in a movement that has gone from nonviolent demonstrations at lunch counters to talk of revolution in a single decade. Bobby Seale and Huey P. Newton represent links in a chain stretching from a peaceful North Carolina college campus to the teeming Oakland ghetto.

It was the Greensboro 4 on February 1, 1960, who gave birth to twentieth-century student activism. Their spontaneous lunch-counter sit-in was the distant genesis of Huey Newton's plan for the Black Panther Party for Self-Defense. Seale is the heir to the early organizing efforts of young blacks and whites in the rural South. He inherits, as his arguments with Judge Hoffman indicate, the demand of the early 60's students that fundamental constitutional guarantees and promises—so long violated by illegitimate white power—be immediately honored, while reserving the right to attack the system itself. Thus the Panthers become the logical extension of the student organizing efforts of the 60's, for the Panthers have carried that organizing into the urban ghetto while discarding the anti-white sentiments that grew in many of the students who were bloodied in race wars in Alabama and Mississippi.

The Panthers face dangers for the future, however. The most obvious is the intense hatred policemen feel toward them, as well as the more sophisticated attacks of FBI Director J. Edgar Hoover and former Attorney General Mitchell. The Panthers will face other Judge Hoffmans in other courtrooms, other police forces in other midnight raids, and will increasingly discover, as Thoreau did, that the state "is not armed with superior wit or honesty, but with superior armed force."

A real, if more subtle, danger is the current lionizing of the

Panthers by the radical, and now increasingly liberal, white communities. It is precisely this marriage that caused the Panthers to condemn SNCC, and they cannot have it both ways. When the radical white community insists, as one of the many sects within SDS did recently, that the Panthers are *"the* vanguard" and that all other groups, therefore, have less revolutionary validity, then the Panthers begin to approach that dangerous abyss in which they are always right and all others are always wrong.

To build more credibility in the black community the Panthers will have to discover a way to expand their appeal beyond "woofing" at policemen, feeding breakfast to children, and providing medical aid for the poor.

Their economic analysis will have to be put into practice as a visible example of the Panthers' ability to deliver on their rhetoric, an ability notoriously lacking in some other black groups.

But in the Seale-Hoffman clash, young black manhood at its most aggressive clashed against Julius Hoffman, the American judiciary at its most moribund, and the judiciary, temporarily, triumphed. It demonstrated, through Seale, that there is in black people an unquenchable desire for freedom from the arbitrary processes that imprison the Bobby Seales, exile the Eldridge Cleavers, murder the Fred Hamptons. These processes, the Panthers try to tell the rest of us, are the same ones that brought slaves here 350 years ago, and are the same processes that inspire the war against the people in Vietnam. These are the processes that the Panthers, in their way, have dedicated themselves to destroy. We had better discover a way, theirs or some other, to join them.

It is hard to measure, even at this vantage point, the final meaning of the Bobby Seale trial.

Contempt cases "have historically been a lightning rod for controversy," as New York University School of Law Professor Norman Dorsen wrote after the Chicago trial was over.

"The mere fact," continued Dorsen, "that the United States Government chose to prosecute carefully selected political leaders in the aftermath of the 1968 Democratic Convention suggested that no ordinary trial would ensue."

And Dorsen offers then another comment that I find interesting and accurate:

> Of course we must not forget . . . that in a case like this, which is but an extension of the political process, defendants like Bobby Seale will naturally regard the courtroom as a symbol of an oppressive "system," and will make their tactical decisions, including their statements to the court, less to influence appellate tribunals than public opinion, or a particular segment of that opinion. This was what Rennie Davis meant when he said that "his jury" would be in the streets the day following the jury verdict in Chicago. It was what I meant earlier in suggesting that the ultimate decision in the case of Bobby Seale and the others must await the judgment of the years and perhaps of persons yet unborn.*

After the court proceedings had ended, Bobby Seale wrote his own "Personal Statement" about what happened. Here are the closing lines:

> Judge Hoffman and the prosecution working together set out from the start to use the difference of manner, dress and general yippie-hippie expression that is associated with youth today. This, of course, was to cloud any real political ideas that criticized the unjustness of the status quo (or rather the Nixon-Agnew-Mitchell fascist puppets of big money) which brought us to trial in the first place. It was also used to cloud any prejudices and seeming unfairness on the part of the court and the prosecution working together against lawyers and defendants. In my case they figured I could be easily railroaded.
>
> A political trial, in which I was drawn by bigoted fascist-racism in government, became a message to the world and especially black

---

* *The "Trial" of Bobby Seale,* ibid.

America. The escalation of fascist state repression (what has been done to black America for countless years) was seen being done to even white youth who are demanding and protesting, rightfully, for the same just society that the hearts, minds, and souls of black people, and brown, red, and other oppressed, have been crying out for and demanding for years.*

What the Panthers do more than anything else for black Americans is that they set a standard of forcefulness that young black people particularly want to measure up to, the sort of standard we haven't had in the past. Our idols have been men like Dr. King, who for all of his beauty as a man, was not that kind of aggressive man, but the Panthers and certainly Malcolm X have set this new kind of standard that a great many young people want to adhere to.

So much has been written and spoken about the Black Panthers in the press and over the radio and TV that one might suppose most people know what the organization really stands for and seeks to achieve. But this is far from the case. Only rarely does the press report what the Panthers are actually saying and doing and how they view the problems of black people in our society. The result is that most Americans have obtained their impression of the Panthers and black people generally from statements issued by those who wish to see them eliminated as a factor in American life.

The language of the Panthers is often shocking to those accustomed to the ordinary expressions of political figures, but we might as well get accustomed to it, for it expresses the sentiments of a vast section of oppressed Americans. The Panthers articulate what the black people feel and, in so doing, enable all of us to gain insight into the deep-set anger of so many of the deprived, as well as into their determination to change these conditions.

As this is written in early 1972, there is another significant political trial pending, that of Angela Yvonne Davis in connection

* *Ibid.*

with the revolt of three black prisoners on August 7, 1970, at the Marin County Courthouse in California. Miss Davis is charged with murder, kidnapping, and conspiracy.

Writing of another political trial, his own, in 1951, W. E. B. Du Bois said:

What turns me cold in all this experience is the certainty that thousands of innocent victims are in jail today because they had neither money, experience nor friends to help them. The eyes of the world were on our trial despite the desperate effort of press and radio to suppress the facts and cloud the real issues; the courage and money of friends and of strangers who dared stand for a principle freed me; but God only knows how many who were as innocent as I and my colleagues are today in hell. They daily stagger out of prison doors embittered, vengeful, hopeless, ruined. And of this army of the wronged, the proportion of Negroes is frightful. We protect and defend sensational cases where Negroes are involved. But the great mass of arrested or accused black folk have no defense. There is desperate need . . . to oppose this national racket of railroading to jails and chain gangs the poor, friendless and black.*

Dr. Du Bois's 1951 observations are twice as true twenty years later, the practice of charging and imprisoning the helpless and the friendless goes on. The "army of the wronged" has increased its ranks: Angela Davis, Ruchell Magee, and the surviving Soledad Brothers are presently its most notable legionnaires.

And Du Bois's point is still valid today, that the celebrated and famous receive our attention; the nonentities and the nameless pass on by.

Angela Davis, Ruchell Magee, and the three Soledad Brothers (become two through George Jackson's murder) are rooted in the progressive forces of our time.

* W. E. B. Du Bois, *The Autobiography of W. E. B. Du Bois.* International Publishers, New York, 1968.

A word about the late George Jackson.

When one reads his letters from prison, the inevitable comparison is with Eldridge Cleaver, another California convict who freed himself from the "slave" mentality while in prison, or even Malcolm X, whose political development began in prison with letters from the Honorable Elijah Muhammad.

But there is something else in Jackson's letters, not sharper, more militant, or more or less anything, but writing and politics not found in Cleaver or Malcolm.

The reader feels the bars and walls and keepers pressing in on Jackson and, through him, on us all. One gets a photo-look at life inside; a far more oppressive picture than we may have thought possible.

Jackson makes it plain and real that the life he lived for ten years in jail is an extension of the life we all live outside, with ruled and rulers, oppressed and oppressors, and the common intermediaries who in prison and out will successfully try to worry one class against another.

Jackson's optimism (". . . in spite of the bitter experience of these years I still find it easy to trust people"), his pride in race and self ("I'm part of a righteous people who anger slowly but rage undammed"), his critique of nonviolence ("nonviolence must constantly demonstrate the effects of its implied opposite"),* and his ups and downs come through in his letters with a clarity and heat.

Surely, here was a man who deserved to be read and heard more, and a man whose untimely death means that the letters are the only way we will ever hear from him. Finally, here was a man.

There is a line from Du Bois to Seale to Jackson and to Angela Davis; a chain exists linking the dark "army of the wronged" that has marched from the loins of black America for the past 350 years. But these named, so familiar to us all, are but the tip of an

---

* George Jackson, *Soledad Brother*. Coward-McCann, New York, 1970.

iceberg, a crag of black bluehard coldness so massive it could sink America.

It will not suffice to mouth slogan and rhetoric. Even Richard Nixon now says "Power to the People." What is wanted for those whose names are known, and for the "army of the wronged" not known by name, is concerted and organized action.

They come from a proud people whose history of struggle against domestic colonialism here is well known. Our dangers lie in our unwillingness to close ranks around the known and the unknown, and our dangerous tendencies to forget the war when single battles are won. Where was the defense committee for Donald Stone? For young Ben Chaney? For Roosevelt Jackson Jones? Where are the millions to march for freedom for those who may never march, except in lock step, again.

They could come from the readers of this book.

X-
Federal Bureau of Intimidation

ONE of the most meaningless campaign promises ever made came from Richard Nixon in 1968 when he repeatedly vowed to attack crime in the streets and restore law and order by firing Attorney General Ramsey Clark.

It was a political punch line that candidate Nixon used both before and after his nomination at the Republican convention in Miami in August. It formed a part of his acceptance speech to the convention on the evening of August 8, 1968.

"If we are to restore order and respect for law in this country, there's one place we're going to begin: we're going to have a new Attorney General of the United States of America."

Columnist Mary McGrory commented on Nixon's use of this punch line, this effort to "personalize" the crime issue, in a column written after the election.

"At every rally, just before the balloons fell down and the candidate shot up his arms in his double-V sign, Nixon would assure his audience that respect for the law would begin at approximately the moment that the nation's chief law-enforcement officer quit the Department of Justice." Nixon's audiences as a rule stomped the floor and shouted approval. Of course, he spoke as a rule only to predictably favorable audiences; when Nixon appeared on supposed question-and-answer television shows, it was in a carefully contrived situation, always, with planted questions and canned answers.

Richard Harris, chronicler of Nixon's version of the law-and-order crisis, suggested that the singling out of Ramsey Clark was a fairly deliberate and calculated tactic, if not one Nixon personally relished.

Apparently, Nixon himself did not enjoy his attacks on the Attorney General. "Ramsey Clark is really a fine fellow," he said to his closest associates during the campaign. "And he's done a good job." In the view of one of the candidate's top advisers, the candidate had felt compelled to use this "simplistic approach" to stir up the voters. But in the view of a former official of the Eisenhower Administration that explanation did not go deep enough. "Whenever Dick finds himself in trouble, he always personalizes an issue," he explained. "In this case, crime was the issue and Clark was the person."*

Nixon's pledge to fire Attorney General Clark had a cynical political meaning but no substance at all from any other point of view.

First of all, firing a particular Cabinet member as a major campaign issue was a faintly ridiculous idea (as serious idea, that is, not as political catchword). Every member of any outgoing President's Cabinet automatically resigns his post, certainly including the Attorney General. Secondly, the Attorney General of the United States has enormous influence in many ways, almost as a symbolic figure, but the Attorney General also has very little direct control of local law enforcement, virtually none, in fact, at

* Richard Harris, *Justice.* E. P. Dutton, New York, 1970. Much of the contents first appeared in *The New Yorker* magazine.

the state and city levels, where law-enforcement agencies deal most directly with "crime in the streets."

In fact, Federal Bureau of Investigation figures on various categories of crime have shown a substantial increase in each of President Nixon's first three years in office.

By the Nixon reasoning, presumably, then, one major step toward law and order would be to kick out Attorney General John Mitchell. Effective March 1, Mitchell resigned to help manage Nixon's 1972 re-election campaign. Maybe, again following the Nixon logic on attorney generals, that will mean a reduction in the crime rate in the last part of 1972.

Such FBI figures on crime, of course, may prove of little value.

As former Attorney General Ramsey Clark wrote, after leaving office, the "crime clock" used by the FBI measures only the frequency of crime reported to police throughout the nation, not the rate of crime based on the whole population.

. . . What does it mean to tell the nation that seven serious crimes are committed each minute of the day, that a murder occurs every thirty-nine minutes, a forcible rape every seventeen minutes, a robbery every two minutes? It means that you take the public for a fool. For how many people are born, how many die, how many homes burn, how many suffer heart attacks, how many are injured in automobile accidents in the same period? If the same frequency for crimes were applied to China with its fourfold greater population, the clock would toll one-fourth the crime per capita it indicates here. If the crimes measured occurred in the Virgin Islands the whole population would be dead of murder in three years, having been previously raped twice and robbed eighteen times.*

Whatever the merit of such FBI figures or of corporate lawyer Mitchell as a crime fighter, one thing was clear under his tenure

* Ramsey Clark, *Crime in America*. Simon and Schuster, New York, 1970.

of office as Attorney General of the United States. It became easy to believe that he was, as widely reported, the chief architect of President Nixon's "Southern strategy," that calculated appeal to white racism, which in reality reached North and South in a cynical bid for votes. It became apparent too that Nixon intended to pursue that strategy again in 1972, as he had in 1968.

The Federal Bureau of Intimidation deserves some special consideration in discussing the attacks made on black Americans. Such attacks have often involved the alleged just enforcers of the law, whether in an Alabama sheriff's office or at a much higher level.

The federal government and the little tyrant who runs the FBI have given notice that they believe they can with impunity listen in on the conversations of anyone in the United States. They have admitted that they planted listening "bugs" in the telephone, the living room, and the automobile of an important religious leader, the Honorable Elijah Muhammad. They have admitted they bugged the telephone conversations and hotel rooms of the late Dr. Martin Luther King, Jr.

The next time you call someone or have a conversation with someone that you think is private, ask yourself whether Attorney General Mitchell or J. Edgar Hoover or someone similar might not be listening in.

We have seen in recent times too a series of vicious and well-coordinated attacks made by local policemen and the FBI on the Black Panther Party, one of the vanguard organizations in the black liberation struggle. Their leaders have been arrested, their offices ransacked. You may not care what happens to the Black Panthers, although you should, but if you don't speak out when the Panthers are attacked, ask yourself, who will speak out for you?

The director of the FBI, J. Edgar Hoover, is a petty bully, a small-bore egomaniac who can't abide criticism either from without or from within his organization. He is an aging boy wonder, one who should have retired years ago.

If I seem to feel strongly about the FBI's role in the struggle for racial justice in this country, it is not without reason. Most of us who were active in civil rights in the South in the 1960's know first hand of instances of civil rights workers being beaten and harassed and pushed around, sometimes with FBI agents actually on the scene taking no action. Or of young civil rights activists abused in small Southern jails, and when the FBI investigated, only under considerable pressure, that FBI investigation consisting of a perfunctory look at the jail itself and a simple question to the jailer or the deputy or the sheriff, Are you abusing these prisoners' civil rights? Why no, of course not, the reply would come, white deputy sheriff peering at white FBI agent in sympathetic communication (for a long while Mr. Hoover kept the FBI one of the most lily-white government preserves).

The FBI, as an agency and institution, has come under fire in the last few years for a number of reasons having nothing to do with civil rights.

For decades, Hoover and other FBI officials insisted that there was no such thing as organized crime in this country. Other law-enforcement agencies were already attempting to face up to such legitimate problems of law and order at the same time that Director Hoover seemed mainly intent on asking Congress for a larger appropriation each year or infiltrating a few more FBI agents into the politically ineffectual Communist Party organization within the United States. One theory holds that the Communist Party in this country would probably have gone bankrupt years ago were it not for the dues paid dutifully by undercover FBI agents.

Former Attorney General Ramsey Clark, who has certainly had his differences with Hoover, is curiously one of the most eloquent defenders of Hoover's long law-enforcement record. While making no secret of their differences, Clark is also inclined to point out that Hoover built an efficient professional agency from an early period when no agency had the high basic professional qualifications that Hoover demanded of his men, and that through the years Hoover has steadfastly resisted the temptation to turn the FBI into a super "national police" agency, even to the point of directly refusing to absorb some other agencies or functions within his organization.

But Clark also had firsthand contact with the FBI and its deficiencies, particularly those involving the Hoover cult of personality within the agency. Attorney General Robert Kennedy, according to Clark, brought a firsthand understanding of organized crime to his department, based on his congressional committee rackets investigation experience, and an intense interest in battling organized crime. The FBI tended to participate less, rather than more, in Kennedy's efforts.

The conflict between Attorney General Kennedy [said Clark] and the FBI arose from the unwillingness of the Bureau to participate on an equal basis with other crime control agencies. The FBI has so coveted personal credit that it will sacrifice even effective crime control before it will share the glory of its exploits. This has been a petty and costly characteristic caused by the excessive domination of a single person, J. Edgar Hoover, and his self-centered concern for his reputation and that of the FBI.*

Hoover's vanity has no doubt done its share of harm to the FBI and that agency's reputation. Yet aside from that, it concerns me that people understand why black Americans, especially in the South, have an often grim impression of the FBI. Frequently, that agency has seemed to work as an affiliate of the local sheriff and police and National Guard in a racially repressive way. Unlike the U.S. Supreme Court in the 1950's and 1960's, or even the White House and the U.S. Congress at certain dramatic points in the 1960's, the FBI as an institution never seemed to ally itself with those struggling for racial justice. Hoover once called the late Dr. Martin Luther King, Jr., a "notorious liar." That was only a

* *Ibid.*

phrase, if an insulting one. But it seemed generally to reflect the aging Hoover's attitude toward the civil rights movement.

The tragedy at Orangeburg, South Carolina, in February of 1968 illustrates as well as any single instance can what I am talking about.

Orangeburg?

I would like to think the name, or the phrase *The Orangeburg Massacre,* has meaning for anyone happening to read this book. My melancholy fear is that this is not the case. The college students killed were black. Their deaths seemed to move in and out of the national consciousness very swiftly, far more swiftly than those at Kent State, where of course the students shot down were white. In other words, somehow, Orangeburg was easy to forget.

But it should not be forgotten.

Thomas F. Pettigrew, Harvard University professor of social psychology, offered a frightening comparison:

On March 21, 1960, a throng of unarmed, protesting Africans marched on a police station in Sharpeville, South Africa. The focus of their demonstrations involved elementary justice, for it was aimed against the bitterly resented requirements for Africans to carry with them at all times identification and permission papers. Yet the tense government police began firing wildly into the crowd. In a matter of seconds, at least seventy-two Africans were killed and two hundred seriously hurt in the blood bath.

On February 8, 1968, a throng of angry, frustrated black-American students faced off heavily armed police on the grounds of their own college campus in Orangeburg, South Carolina. The focus of their demonstrations also involved elementary justice, for it was aimed against the exclusion of blacks from a local bowling alley. Yet the tense police began firing wildly into the unarmed crowd. In a matter of seconds, there was an American blood bath.

The parallels between Sharpeville and Orangeburg are chilling and undeniable. But they break down in one major respect. The Sharpeville Massacre entered the annals of world infamy, and

March 21, 1970, witnessed memorial observances around the globe a decade later. It was accurately and widely reported; and it was responded to in a manner befitting the event. Even the United States Department of State, not noted for its critical actions toward South Africa, issued an unprecedented statement of condemnation. In sharp contrast, the Orangeburg Massacre, if it were heard about in the first place is barely remembered by the world . . .*

The mass media seemed almost to ignore the killings on a black college campus in Orangeburg. *Time* magazine didn't see fit to mention it. The Associated Press, in its initial report, made an incredible blunder, reporting that the students were exchanging gunfire with police. The erroneous report came apparently from an AP photographer who later denied that that was what he said. The AP corrected its later stories by omitting the error but never felt it necessary to make a specific correction that might have helped eliminate the confusion as to what had really happened. There is a world of difference between students killed in an exchange of gunfire and students shot down, most of them shot in the back, the buttocks, and the soles of their feet, while running in terror from police officers who have lost control and begun shooting at unarmed people.

The best account of what really happened at Orangeburg is undoubtedly in a book by two excellent reporters, Jack Nelson and Jack Bass, who covered the initial events for their newspapers, the Los Angeles *Times* and the Charlotte *Observer*. The two painstakingly interviewed dozens of people involved, those directly on the scene and those with knowledge of the racial tensions leading up to the murders on campus and of the aftermath.

I was not in Orangeburg on the night of the killings, but I came later to have one personal involvement. After the killings, South

* Thomas F. Pettigrew, Foreword to *The Orangeburg Massacre,* by Jack Nelson and Jack Bass. World Publishing Company, New York, 1970.

Carolina officials tried to blame snipers and outside agitators for what had happened. They never produced a sniper. There was some indication that firing had been heard from the college campus earlier in the evening. The overwhelming evidence was, however, that no one had fired at law-enforcement officers just before the heavy gunfire began and that no one was firing back at the state patrolmen who were shooting at the backs of fleeing students. Not a single patrolman was struck by gunfire. As "outside agitator," South Carolina settled for Cleveland Sellers.

I knew Sellers, an energetic and honest young man, active both in civil rights and in the peace movement. He had refused to step forward for induction and was charged with violating the selective service law. His trial in March of 1968 came just seven weeks after the Orangeburg shootings, and I was among those appearing in federal court as a character witness for him.

Sellers was hardly responsible for the police riot of Orangeburg.

That Orangeburg story is worth dwelling upon, and I recommend the book by Nelson and Bass. But, here, I am more specifically interested in making the role of the FBI clear.

Three young men died in the shooting itself: Henry Ezekial Smith, Delano Herman Middleton, and Samuel Hammond, Jr. Their names should be recorded here, if only in memoriam. "I am living a relatively normal Christian life. I am going to church more than I did last year. I am trying to do unto others as I would have them do unto me. I think that is about all God can ask of a person," Henry Smith wrote to his mother, in his last letter home, six days before he was killed, a letter of a typical college student, penciled on a piece of tablet paper. My point here is only that the three young men killed were not strangers or outside agitators or depraved beings. They, and the other students shot and only wounded, were fairly ordinary young Americans who happened to be black and who happened to be protesting against racial discrimination.

Not long after the shooting, a black educator, thirty-four-year-old President Benjamin F. Payton of Benedict College in Columbia, addressed a Columbia civic club, the first Negro to address a major civic club in that city. He is a graduate of South Carolina State College, where the students were killed, and had gone on to compile a distinguished academic record, with graduate degrees from Yale, Harvard, and Columbia. Payton posed a question to the civic club:

"Was it necessary that three people be killed because one hundred of them threw bricks? I have difficulty conceiving in my imagination of the highway patrolmen firing point-blank at students of the University of South Carolina or Clemson doing the same thing."*

The primary investigation of the killings was undertaken by the U.S. Justice Department, rather than the FBI. Chief J. P. Strom of the State Law Enforcement Division was sometimes known as South Carolina's J. Edgar Hoover, and it soon became apparent that the nickname had special meaning in the sense of a close working relationship between the FBI and South Carolina law-enforcement officials.

Deputy Assistant Attorney General D. Robert Owen, second-highest official in the civil rights division, sought out Charles DeFord, FBI agent in charge in Columbia on February 10. He found him staying at the Holiday Inn in Orangeburg, sharing a room with Chief Strom.

Perhaps most incredible was that three FBI agents were actually on the scene at the time of the shootings. Yet the Justice Department officials investigating the whole thing were not informed of this fact. They learned of it almost accidently three months later. The FBI had even submitted a written report of its Orangeburg investigation two months after the events without mentioning that three of their agents had been eyewitnesses. It is interesting in this same connection to note that South Carolina officials said publicly, quite early, that they were sure the FBI investigation would clear their patrolmen of any wrongdoing.

* Jack Nelson and Jack Bass, *The Orangeburg Massacre*. World Publishing Co., New York, 1970.

Nine patrolmen were eventually tried on charges arising from the Orangeburg murders, the first case in the nation involving the use of excessive police power in controlling college campus demonstrations. They were acquitted. The defense frequently emphasized how closely their state and local law-enforcement officers worked with the FBI.

XI-
The Establishment

THERE IS a great deal of discussion in the United States today, especially among the young and the alienated, of several words that have already become clichés. Those most commonly used are probably the words "system" and "Establishment."

It is supposed, by those who use these terms, that the Establishment may be either very large or very small and may include both Nelson Rockefeller and the late Whitney Young, Jr., and, in the minds of some, even the late Dr. Martin Luther King, Jr. It may include only a few supermillionaires or even the entire American middle class. But it is, in the minds of those who use the expression, certainly the group that controls things in the United States, and, in fact, much of the rest of the world.

The system is more easily but still loosely defined, however; it is the process that keeps the Establishment in power. Questions are raised about the system, however, as to whether it serves the Establishment because it is flawed and nonfunctioning, or whether it has been purposely designed, by that same Establishment, to perform as it does and is, in fact, working perfectly.

That is a subject for another day, however. For the moment, let us consider the vague organization, the Establishment, its relationship to white and to a great many black young people, and the likelihood or even probability of it becoming either moderately or radically different than it is today. One may assume that if such an animal exists, black Americans are as a people certainly oppressed by it, and if the Establishment depends on capitalism and corporate liberalism and moderate welfare democracy for its existence, then they too must be challenged if our oppression is to end.

The props that support this Establishment must be attacked simply because there is no option, given the nature of the oppression emanating from it, in exchanging a white set of oppressors for a black set. That is why schemes like "black capitalism" have not caught on in the black community; that is why some young black people are currently pursuing a formal education but rejecting the normal success-oriented goal of it.

Black people have always existed—and barely at that—at the sufferance of the Establishment of the United States. That was true more than one hundred years ago, when the Civil War ended and black Americans thought we would have a chance at determining our own destiny. It has happened again, more recently, at the end of a similar era of hope and limited progress.

What is happening now happened once before in American history in the years after Reconstruction. The promises that black people would be included in the social and economic life of the nation were repudiated. Instead of fulfilling the dream, then and now:

—The white crusaders for social justice and democracy became weary as black people could no longer be considered a purely Southern problem;

—The aspirations for and movement of blacks began to be curtailed by organized violence and barbarity and by a series of legal maneuvers designed to make black men less than political and economic equals;

—The hopes and belief of black people that racial equality and social justice could be achieved through litigation, legislation, negotiation, occasional direct action and strong alliances with white liberal groups were supplanted by disillusionment, bitterness, and open anger;

—The guilt and indignation of Northern supporters of the Southern drive for equality turned into an attitude of cautious—and now open—racism when the Northern black man began to take seriously the claims of progress and began to look for visible signs in Northern cities.*

Those who directed and helped staff the movement from lunch counters to bus stations to voting booths to electoral politics are no longer there. Those Northerners whose concern and whose money helped finance that movement are no longer concerned or financing. The government we once thought mildly sympathetic to our goals is no longer the government and is certainly no longer sympathetic.

The nation that spent $30 billion a year to interfere in the political future of over eighteen million Vietnamese and less than one-tenth that amount to insure a decent future for twenty-seven million poor black and white Americans has now said, in effect, that even though the war ends completely, there will be nothing like that $30 billion spent for domestic affairs, for, say, the pressing needs of the poor.

It has been class versus class and race versus race in this country from the seventeenth century to this one. It probably will continue to be that. What is discussible and important to discuss today is not whether but how the question will be put in the future. What responses will those in power make? Will the Establishment once more absorb, as it does so well, those who rail against it?

The question of race will be increasingly put to the Establishment in violent terms. This will not be the heated mass violence of Watts and Detroit and Newark, but rather the violence that came

---

* Paraphrased, in part, from a speech by Dr. Kenneth Clark to the Southern Regional Council.

to terrorize draft centers, the violence that has every big-city white policeman nervous and jumpy. In effect the natives, some few of them, a small, small number, are becoming guerrillas and the colonial administrators are becoming worried.

For the future, despite the urging or condemnation by anyone, violence will ensue. The day of wholesale looting and burning has passed, not because radical changes resulted from it, but because it is easier to attack two policemen at a time than it is to battle two hundred; it is easier and less costly in human life to destroy a downtown credit-reference bureau than it is to single out and destroy its colonial outpost in the ghetto. The records are downtown and not in the ghetto, anyway.

While this activity occurs, and it is occurring now, every week in some part of the country, more ordinary actions will be occurring as well. This is to say that the whole range of black activism will continue, from picket lines to voter registration drives to student disruptions to marches to draft refusals and to every other form of protest tried during the last decade.

What will be different in the future, however, is not just that black men want the blue-collar security of a union card or that young black people want a formal college education, but that the young and some of the old, both black and white, are determined to follow the slogan of Eldridge Cleaver, ". . . if you are not part of the solution, you are part of the problem." And none of them wants now, or ever, to be a part of the problem.

Some will be, of course: the rewards of moderation are too great; the difficulty of the struggle is too exacting. But there is, on the campus and in the streets, a new breed of young people for whom a generation gap is not twenty or twenty-five years, but from this year's graduating class to the next. The National Student Association recently found that during two months of a single school year sixteen thousand college students had been arrested for smoking marijuana. Smoking pot is far from revolutionary action, but it is anti-Establishment, and I suggest that the sixteen thousand is a small and visible tip of a large and hidden iceberg.

This iceberg, unlike others, gets larger, rather than smaller, and it includes not just those who have dates with Mary Jane, but those who have decided not to accept, and to show that they do not accept, the same old bill of goods.

The war in Vietnam to them is not an aberration that has lately gone wrong; for them, and they are correct, it never was right. White racism, to them, has been an American constant, not something that was discovered by Senator Fred Harris and Mayor John Lindsay and former Governor Kerner; sex is something to be enjoyed, outdoors in the middle of the street, if you will, and not a hidden exercise in guilt.

The violence and the mindlessness that accompany these ideas might not be attractive, but they can never equal the violence dispensed by those on what is called the other side.

So these young people may continue to grow in numbers as they discover that the old ways don't work. They are not the first generation to make this discovery, but they are certainly the first generation to begin on a wide scale the process of withdrawal from Establishment ranks while attempting to construct their own alternative to it. They are, it is said, constructing their own Establishment, but surely it will not and cannot be the same thing. Surely it will aim away from profit-oriented labor and toward a new and yet undefined ethic that will insist on putting into practice what is now merely a slogan, "Doing your own thing."

A French student in Paris chants: "We are all German Jews." A black girl at Tougaloo College in Mississippi writes: "The sharecropper is me, the domestic is me."

They, these young people, are determined to make a better world or know the reason why. They are determined, and they are marching straight from the pages of Tom Hayden's testimony not too long ago before the U.S. House Committee on Un-American Activities.

We are going to win either way [Hayden said]. The Chicago Convention brutality was a tremendous kind of victory for the young people of this country who are not voters, people who are not polled by Gallup or Harris, but people who do watch television, and who do not identify with the young Nixon girls or David Eisenhower, but identify with the young people in the streets, and who watch very carefully. If you think you have had militant people before you in these hearings, you have yet to see what the seven- and eight-year-olds are going to bring you in the next five to ten years.

You have taught them to have no respect for authority, and that is a victory in the sense that committees like yourselves are through. You exist only formally; you exist officially, but you have lost all authority, and when a group of people who have power lose their authority, they have lost. You have lost. Period.

I believe that is the proper epitaph—if premature—for the Establishments in this country. They have lost. Period.

XII-

The Kent State Massacre

ON MAY 4, 1970, there was murder done on the Kent State college campus. On that day, four students were brutally and almost at random shot down by National Guard gunfire. Ten students were wounded, also at random.

Ten days after the Kent State killings, another set of murders occurred in Jackson, Mississippi, at another college. There are many like myself who will always believe that if those killed in Jackson had to die at all, they were lucky to die when they did, right after Kent, so that someone besides their classmates, their mothers, and their teachers would know that they lived and died at all.

The four students murdered by National Guard fire at Kent State were white, you see; the other police murders in Jackson involved black students.

The killing of white college students stirred considerable momentary outrage, though it should be said not in the local community in Portage County, Ohio, where Kent State is located. A grand jury there completely exonerated the National Guardsmen of any blame or fault in those deaths and instead indicted—would you believe?—twenty-five other people, students and nonstudents and one professor from the college. That spectacle came to a sorry end in 1971 when, of the first five brought to trial, two pleaded guilty, two were cleared, and charges were dismissed against the fifth. Then charges were dropped for the remaining twenty after hanging over their heads for more than a year. Presumably the National Guardsmen who killed the students continue to draw their weekend warrior pay and no doubt some have been promoted since May of 1970.

Alas, those grand jury indictments are all too easy to believe. Just as it is easy to believe that Attorney General Mitchell would drop federal investigation of the murders in August of 1971, as he indeed did. More than ten thousand Kent State students signed petitions to President Nixon asking that the investigation continue. To no avail, perhaps needless to say. One of the twenty-five indicted commented gloomily when the charges were finally tried in the Portage County courthouse: "You can't maintain your outrage for a year. Now everyone has his own trip: dope, work or the counter-culture."*

Maybe that numbness of spirit after a time is the real message of Kent State.

But that is all history now and we, like good students, are pre-determined to either learn from it and move ahead or are doomed to repeat it again and again. Repeating it means more than Guardsmen and dead bodies and bloodthirsty policemen on college campuses; it means that we will never get free from the trap that has been set for us, the trap that shows movement and agitation rising and ebbing and rising and now ebbing again.

In those terms, Kent State was a high-water mark. It signaled a new kind of rage on the campus, among many of the young who had chosen not to be enraged before. At Kent State in 1970, bullets ceased to discriminate, just as billy clubs stopped discriminating in Chicago in 1968. But that rage was never translated into any kind of movement, demonstrating that rage generated by instant death is perhaps not sufficient to sustain an orderly,

---

* *Time,* December 6, 1971, p. 21.

disciplined attack on the oppression and wrong that generated that death.

What will it take to build and sustain a determined attempt literally to overthrow the grip held on all of the oppressed people living within our nation's shores, as well as those just now beginning their struggle around the globe? What is immediately obvious is how it cannot be done. It cannot be done by adventurism of the sort that results in appealing rhetoric but also in increased repression for this country's nonwhite population. Revolution is seldom precipitated through exercise of the vocal cords, and slander, however clever, will never substitute for rational analysis.

Woodstockism cannot be tolerated while Watts exists; military science on the campus as an *issue* cannot compete for the attention of today's activist with rats in the ghetto. Debates about the revisionism of Ho Chi Minh or Tito are hardly affordable in a land with no revolutionary ideology of its own. It is not simply that these things are unequal but that one has no place beside the other; it is foolish to ask a people whose daily preoccupation is with survival to appreciate the niceties of North Korea's position on women's rights or whether the Army discriminates against homosexuals or whether Tide pollutes more than Ivory Snow.

Survival is precisely the question for all of America's underclass, and particularly so for black people. Every current statistic suggests that we are gradually sinking into a pathological state induced by our constant position at the bottom of the American heap. And every current study and analysis demonstrates that despite whatever minimal achievements we have struggled through over the last decade, our position in relation to everyone else is getting worse.

We blacks come to this point in 1972 through a peculiar history, made peculiar not just by color and condition and previous and present servitude, but through the often confusing availability of differing sets of alternatives. It is important to try to understand the alternatives not only of the present but of the immediate past.

The black struggle of the last decades can be divided into two distinct periods. Bayard Rustin described the periods eloquently in an article in *Harper's* magazine.

I have some disagreement with his suggestions for what must happen in the future, but little disagreement is possible with his perceptive analysis of what has occurred in the past, especially in the critical decade of the 1960's. Let me quote him at some length and then try to indicate where I differ about the course the future will take. Rustin wrote:

. . . The first phase, which covered something like the first half of the decade, was one in which the movement's clear objective was to destroy the legal foundations of racism in America. Thus the locale of the struggle was the South, the evil to be eliminated was Jim Crow, and the enemy, who had a special talent for arousing moral outrage among even the most reluctant sympathizers with the cause, was the rock-willed segregationist.

Now, one thing about the South more than any other has been obscured in the romantic vision of the region—of ancient evil, of defeat, of enduring rural charm—that has been so much of our literary and intellectual tradition; for the Negro, Southern life had precisely a quality of clarity, a clarity which while oppressive was also supportive. The Southern caste system and folk culture rested upon a clear, albeit unjust, set of legal and institutional relationships which prescribed roles for individuals and established a modicum of social order. The struggle that was finally mounted against the system was actually fed and strengthened by the social environment from which it emerged. No profound analysis, no overriding social theory was needed in order both to locate and understand the injustices that were to be combatted. All that was demanded of one was sufficient courage to demonstrate against them. One looks back upon this period in the civil-rights movement with nostalgia.

During the second half of the Sixties, the center of the crisis shifted to the sprawling ghettos of the North. Here black experience was radically different from that of the South. The stability of institutional relationships was largely absent in Northern ghettos, especially among the poor. Over twenty years ago, the black sociologist E. Franklin Frazier was able to see the brutalizing effect of urbanization upon lower-class blacks: ". . . the bonds of sympathy and community of interests that held their parents together in the rural environment have been unable to withstand the disintegrating forces in the city." Southern blacks migrated north in search of work, seeking to become transformed from a peasantry into a working class. But instead of jobs they found only misery, and far from becoming a proletariat, they came to constitute a *Lumpenproletariat,* an underclass of rejected people. Frazier's prophetic words resound today with terrifying precision: ". . . as long as the bankrupt system of Southern agriculture exists, Negro families will continue to seek a living in the towns and cities of the country. They will crowd the slum areas of Southern cities or make their way to Northern cities, where their family life will become disrupted and their poverty will force them to depend upon charity."

Out of such conditions, social protest was to emerge in a form peculiar to the ghetto, a form which could never have taken root in the South except in such large cities as Atlanta or Houston. The evils in the North are not easy to understand and fight against, or at least not as easy as Jim Crow, and this has given the protest from the ghetto a special edge of frustration. There are few specific injustices, such as a segregated lunch counter, that offer both a clear object of protest and a good chance of victory. Indeed, the problem in the North is not one of social injustice so much as the results of institutional pathology. Each of the various institutions touching the lives of urban blacks—those relating to education, health, employment, housing and crime—is in need of drastic reform. One might say that the Northern race problem has in good part become simply the problem of the American city—which is gradually becoming a reservation for the unwanted, most of whom are black . . .

If the problems of the ghetto do not lend themselves to simple analyses or solutions, then, this is because they cannot be solved without mounting a total attack on the inadequacies endemic to, and injustices embedded in, all of our institutions. . . .*

Rustin then sums up where we are and what we face by stating that the truth about the Negro's situation in America today:

is that there are powerful forces, composed largely of the corporate elite and Southern conservatives, which will resist any change in the economic or racial structure of this country that might cut into their resources or challenge their status; and such is precisely what any program genuinely geared to improve his lot must do. Moreover, these forces today are not merely resisting change. With their representative Richard Nixon in the White House, they are engaged in an assault on the advances made during the past decade. It has been Nixon's tragic and irresponsible choice to play at the politics of race, not, to be sure, with the primitive demagoguery of a "Pitchfork Ben" Tillman, say, but nevertheless with the same intent of building a political majority on the basis of white hostility to blacks. So far he has been unsuccessful, but the potential for the emergence of such a reactionary majority does exist, especially if the turbulence and racial polarization which we have recently experienced persists.

What is needed, therefore, is not only a program that would effect some fundamental change in the distribution of America's resources for those in the greatest need of them, but also a political majority that will support such a program. . . .†

Here we part company, Rustin and I, as solid as his basic analysis is. His analysis suggests a partial escape from the circle of a politics that always escalates into protests, culminates in rebellion, and results in repression.

But I see no present likelihood or even any possibility of a program for basic change in the nation's economic system, or a

* Bayard Rustin, "The Blacks and the Unions," *Harper's,* May 1971.
† *Ibid.*

change in the distribution of resources, that could come close to commanding a political majority. What is possible, I think, is the construction of a political movement that can seize some power in the standard civics-textbook fashion of electoral victory after electoral victory, while in parallel fashion it allows for the growing nationalist sentiment that the American black community is now pregnant with. This pregnancy can be stillborn or aborted if majority America reinforces the concentration-camp and reservation psychosis that is slowly throttling our native-born colonial population. Or it could give birth to the kind of ethnic diversity that we at present so falsely insist our pluralistic society permits.

Such a political movement need not be built only on economic considerations, or even as Rustin put it, the need for a fundamental change in the distribution of resources in America. There may be many issues. Black Americans, in particular, must be aware that they need coalitions to win electoral victories. There are major cities, some congressional districts, and other communities where the electorate is made up of 50 per cent black voters or close to it. But in most communities and states, and nationally, there is both the need and the possibility for coalition politics.

The murders of students at Kent State and Jackson State were not enough to galvanize college students in a serious political direction. But the possibility of a new majority politics in America rests with these students and those like them across the nation, black and white. And I would say to these students: If politics depresses you, consider that when the Cuban people overthrew Batista, they brought about political change; and as the Vietnamese continue their centuries-old struggle to be free of foreign domination, they are undergoing political change.

Young Americans may long for this sort of activism and militant and military manner, but they should remember what Che Guevara said (it seems so many years ago), "The streets of Harlem are not the mountains of the Sierra Maestre."

It is particularly important that young people involve themselves in political activism in the broadest spectrum. This is not simply election-day doorbell ringing, but the more important task of building constituencies of common interest that can force change through their votes, through their measured feet marching in the streets, or through whatever form of mass action they—not we—choose to undertake.

It is important for them because it offers a chance at what black people have been asking for 350 years; a chance to have something to say about what is being done to us, or about us.

It is also important because these young people could offer some life and hope to a people without hope who are close to spiritual and political death, and it is important because just over two years ago, after Kent State, many promised they would do something and then did nothing at all.

Most of us will do nothing anyway, no matter how many speeches are made or how many shots are fired or bodies counted or babies starve to death. But it remains important because, since our mothers and fathers didn't do it, and if we fail to do it, our children may not have a chance at it.

George Wald, a Nobel laureate in physiology and medicine, stated what might be the theme of a new political movement: "Our business is with life, not death. Our challenge is to give what account we can of what becomes of life in the solar system, this corner of the universe that is our home; and most of all, what becomes of men—all men, of all nations, colors and creeds. This has become one world, a world for all men. It is only such a world that can now offer us life, and the chance to go on."*

* George Wald, in a speech at Howard University, March 4, 1969.

XIII-
Lincoln Revisited

THE MORE things change, sometimes, it seems, the more they remain the same. Abraham Lincoln, the President who grudgingly freed the slaves, might well view the racist policies of the modern Republican Party, the party he led, with a grim and almost disbelieving eye. Yet there is one great constant in modern America, whatever else has changed in more than a century, that Lincoln would recognize. It is important that we recognize it too. One cannot discuss what life was like in the 1960's or what it will be like in the 1970's without discussing what appear to be two continuing factors in American life, race and war.

The war in Southeast Asia, with little possibility even yet of any conclusive end, has been a fact of American life for better than two decades; growing concern about the condition of the nonwhite peoples of this country, at least concern on their part, has been the Number One item on the domestic priority list of both the 1960's and 1970's.

These two frightening facts, the one because it could threaten international annihilation, the other because it threatens domestic genocide, color our lives.

They are a reflection of everything else American; the sorry condition of our cities; the dependence of one-tenth of our labor force on war spending; the reactionary stance of the United States Congress; the election of "law and order" candidates; the incredible hunger and malnutrition in the richest country on earth.

There is no escaping the connection in a country where more money is spent on pet food than on food stamps; where private citizens spend more on tobacco than all government does on education; where airlines and rail lines receive income supplements; where farmers receive welfare payments in the hundreds of millions of dollars a year; where the oil industry in the past ten years received government handouts of upward of $50 billion and where supplements for the poor are laughed out of Congress; where 5 per cent of the people have 20 per cent of the wealth and 20 per cent of the people have 5 per cent of the wealth. There can be no denial that we are a generation of people who may be without a future; we may be living on the edge of domestic as well as worldwide chaos that may destroy us all.

It cannot be a mistake that the Communist Party of the Soviet Union and many American capitalists make the same analysis of the United States. That analysis suggests that this country has to maintain its present grip on the economies of the underdeveloped nations of the world or we shall have to lower our standard of living. It may be true that consumption will have to be changed in this nation, both in order to redistribute what there is to be consumed and also in order to have something to be consumed, but it is also true that our preserving this economic advantage is done at a prohibitive cost.

"We cannot afford continued imperialism, either financially or spiritually, without the nation ceasing to function as a democratic state," as Richard J. Barnet wrote in *The Economy of Death*.

The United States of America makes up 6 per cent of the world's population; each year we consume 60 per cent of the earth's consumable resources. This fact constitutes the only real threat from the undeveloped world. To imagine that the Vietnamese peasants who have been successfully resisting domination of their land from any quarter for several hundred years are going to attack Honolulu in concert with the revolutionaries from Cuba is to imagine that the United States constitutes a real threat to all the nations that have expressed a real desire to govern themselves. If we do constitute that threat, then the fear is real; if the fear is real, we had better try to dispel it in a way radically different from the gunboat diplomacy of the past.

But it is precisely this concern with the revolutionary activity of the rice farmers of Southeast Asia and the cane cutters and tin miners of South America that has taken our attention from the more serious threat from within. This is not the obviously absurd threat that a minority of black people will somehow overthrow the government of the United States, but that the age-old division of black and white and rich and poor will become so deep that no bringing together will be possible, that the two separate societies so long in existence will continue indefinitely each year more closely resembling colonizer and colonized.

To suggest that these two problems can be attacked separately is to believe one is not a function of the other; no nation that cares for its people can make war on another; no nation that cares about the dignity of all men could let the people of its own soil exist as some of the people of this nation do.

One solution would suggest that the system functions well enough, but that it is run now by corrupt men; that representative democracy as we know it can work, but it has somehow gone astray; that people are basically good, but have been led down the wrong path. If that were true, then we would have a simple task indeed; an army of young people and others toppled one President in 1968; that same army could be reconstituted, we could topple this one and many of his underlings, replace them with decent people, and our new world would be secure.

But a good system would work well no matter how imperfect the men in it, and radical change in American foreign and domestic policy requires a simple reconstitution of the instruments of power.

The decision-making process that decides to build one anti-ballistic missile costing $11 billion needs to be reordered. For the dollar price paid for that one piece of already obsolete hardware, 400,000 units of low-cost housing or 400,000 schoolrooms or 1,300 hospitals could be purchased.

These are not powers vested solely in Congress, but in the bureaucratic agencies of government that change little from President to President. The assumptions and the men who govern their actions vary little from year to year. These must be radically altered if the quality of life in this country is to be altered as well.

Could not the $125,000 that Senator Eastland has been paid in a single year for not planting cotton have been better spent in resettling dispossessed black people on that unused land?

Could not the energy spent in destroying villages thousands of miles away go into building villages here?

We have heard that the decade of the 1970's will bring promise and progress for all Americans; statesmen and politicians alike tell us these ten years will be *the* ten years in which the United States truly lives up to its declarations, and the years in which the land of the slave becomes the home of the free.

Now this may very well be so, but the experience of the last ten years hardly suggests that it will.

This doesn't mean that man is not a perfectible animal or that he cannot undertake to correct the centuries of wrong heaped upon men and nations by other men and nations; it is to suggest that some learning from past history will have to be absorbed before a real new future can begin.

To be sure, our system of government, representative democracy, has undergone some improvements and reforms since it was first instituted. From the days when the right to vote, and thereby participate in government, was limited to white male property owners, we have seen the franchise enlarged to include women and, all too slowly, black people. From the days when rural America was majority America, we have seen the slow shift to proper representation on a one-man, one-vote basis.

But to believe that these reforms have brought true democracy to this country, or that simply granting the right to vote to every citizen makes for a responsible and responsive government, is to overstate incredibly the case for continuing business as usual.

These last ten years have demonstrated time and time again how people of the nation, rather than the government of the nation, have had to move to get the action they deserved, expected, needed, and were supposed to have by law.

It wasn't until the beginning of the 1960's that four young black men in Greensboro, North Carolina, took what ought to be considered the first step in bringing a much abused phrase, participatory democracy, to reality. They had been preceded, of course, by the thousands of black people in Montgomery, Alabama, who in 1956 voted with their feet against segregated seating in that city's bus lines, but the action of the Greensboro 4 mobilized an unwilling nation into action, spurred a generation of young people to the streets, developed a new consciousness in black communities, and set the example for the rising aggressiveness among college youth.

From lunch counters to bus seats to voting booths to student confrontations to the Eugene McCarthy campaign in 1968 to convention demonstrations—these have been the manifestations of citizen involvement on the left hand of the spectrum. On the right, we have seen the people's politics in the campaign of Wallace of Alabama, the growing militance of white firemen and policemen, the reactionary resistance to job equality from white workingmen. In the middle of the spectrum, we have seen the growing consumer awareness of the American housewife, the frustration of the disappearing small farmer, the new aggressiveness of middle- and low-income workers.

All of these people differ in their motives and their goals.

Some are driven by fear and selfishness; others are caught in an economic system never meant for their benefit; but all are caught up in believing with every good reason that government does not care for them or listen to their opinions. Taken together, although their political differences argue against their ever being together, they constitute a noisy American majority of people who, if they acted together, could shake the foundations of the nation.

The problem for those interested in political change by political action is how to get these people to act in concert—to vote together, let us say, or to march together, or to demonstrate in political unison that they seek common solutions to their common problem, the inhumanity of twentieth-century American life and the domestic brutality that results from a brutal and bankrupt foreign policy.

To suggest that there is an easy answer to the problem of bringing these together constitutes fraud. It will not be done by dismissing blue-collar workers as simple racists who vote for George Wallace; a great many voted for Robert Kennedy as well.

It will not be done by suggesting that one group, America's black people, acting alone can bring about its own deliverance; no group of people with our social identification and relative lack of power can accomplish that task.

It might be done by reminding ourselves again of other words of George Wald:

About two million years ago, man appeared. He has become the dominant species on the earth. All other living things, animal and plant, live by his sufferance. He is the custodian of life on earth, and in the solar system. It's a big responsibility.

The thought that we're in competition with Russians and Chinese is all a mistake and trivial. We are one species, with a world to win. There's life all over this universe, but the only life on the solar system is on earth, and in the whole universe we are the only men.*

If a new sort of movement, a black movement, springs from the active protests and organizing drives of the early 60's, it must be

---

* Wald, *ibid.*

first of all democratic. It must extend to every member of the black community the opportunity to have a say in who gets what from whom. It must cast its votes in a unit, it must deal with problems on a local, regional, national, and international basis, and it must decide that freedoms not enjoyed in Watts or Sunflower County cannot be enjoyed in Westchester County.

It must declare itself in the interest of laboring people, but not become the mistress of organized labor.

It has to seek out its natural allies in the Spanish-speaking community, but must not close its eyes to potential allies in middle-class suburbia.

It must pay attention to a street light in a fifty-foot alley as well as to national legislation involving millions of people and international complications that involve the future of the world.

It must maintain a militance and an aggressiveness that will earn it the respect of those it hopes to lead.

If there are any rules peculiar to this new movement in politics, they would be these outlined by Lerone Bennett in *The Negro Mood.*

1. That social, economic, educational, political, and physical segregation and discrimination fill a very real need for the white majority.

2. That appeals to justice and fair play are outmoded and useless when power, financial gain, and prestige are at stake.

3. That positions of segregation and discrimination will be adhered to until change is forced through coercion, threats, power, or violence.

4. That initiative for black political education and organization must come from within the Negro community and must be sustained on a day-by-day basis.

5. That the geographical distribution of Negroes makes Negro-white coalitions desirable, but only when based on racial self-interest and genuine equality between the coalescing groups.

6. That racial self-interest, race consciousness, and racial soli-

darity must always be paramount in the deeds and words of the black political animal; when self-interest is forgotten, organized racism will continue to dominate and frustrate the best-organized political actions of any black political unit, and will leave it powerless and defenseless.

This new movement must address itself to solving America's white problem, to developing a new sophistication and consciousness in the black and white communities, and in making democracy safe for the world.

Peaceful protests—and the bloodied heads of anonymous thousands—have won the lunch-counter seat, the bus-station bench, the integrated toilet, and the vote. The vote and concentrated, united political action can be a tool for further, more meaningful gains, the gains that fill bellies and build homes and schools, but only if we reject the dangerous sort of equality that we may be winning today.

That equality gives us an equal chance to be poor, an equal chance to be unemployed, an equal chance to drop out of school, and a more than equal chance to fight for someone else's freedom thousands of miles from home.

That equality must be suppressed and replaced with an equality that provides full employment, guaranteed incomes, and makes the American nightmare the American dream.

Only when we have gotten ourselves together, only when we shall have decided who our enemies are and where the battleground ought to be, only when we know in our hearts we are right, and only when we demand that our worst off are treated as well as white America's best off will we begin to see whether this system and this method can make a difference in our lives.

Having done all that, having built a new movement, having forged a new majority coalition, having put people in motion, one further thing will be needed, from black and white, rich and poor alike.

That one further thing is something simple. It is what high-school and college graduation speakers urge upon their charges. It is called commitment.

If we truly commit ourselves, and do it by whatever means and with whatever allies are available, then we may be in a position to seek more ambitious goals for ourselves; then we may be in a position to make the American dream indeed stop being a nightmare.

As Frederick Douglass once said: "Men may not get all they pay for in the world, but they certainly pay for all they get. If we ever get free from the oppression and wrongs heaped upon us, we must pay for their removal. We must do this by labor, by suffering, by sacrifice, and if need be, by our lives and the lives of others."

XIV—

Black Faces in High Places

A RECENT STUDY reported that going into the Presidential election year of 1972 there were roughly 1,800 black elected officials in the United States. That is a small number, to be sure, but it does mean that the number of black people in the United States who practice the art of politics is increasing.

This art is not the art of the possible; for black people, most things are impossible. It is not the art of compromise; for black people, the compromise is always so complete that nothing is left when we are through. No, for black people, this art means simply the process of seeing who gets how much of what from whom.

Although the practice of politics is increasingly scorned today in this country, among black and white, rich and poor, I find it increasingly satisfying. It is a pleasure to be a politician. It is a pleasure because of tradition—it is the world's second-oldest profession—and it is a pleasure because of what that word has come to mean to me and to other practicing black politicians in this country.

I suppose I have met, attended meetings with, had conversations with, and often talked late into the night with a goodly majority of the 1,800 black politicians now holding elective office in the United States. In no way do I pretend to speak for all these officials; no one can really do that. But I have made some observations about them. If you are one of the 1,800 black politicians, in the sense I use the word, then a group of people, most of them black, got together and elected you. They chose you because they believed you could do something for them.

I assume, incidentally, that it was black people who chose the 1,800 because white people, generally speaking, haven't yet learned to separate the man from his race. While black people are always having to choose between two white candidates for president, or for governor, mayor, alderman, or sheriff, if given the choice between white and black, the White Bloc Vote votes its race every time. Black voters have, at least until now, tended to support qualified white candidates even against qualified black candidates (e.g., in the last Atlanta mayor's race, black votes split close to 50-50 in such a situation).

I assume also that the people who chose the 1,800 are similar to the people who chose me. They live in a city or a town; they live in what outsiders call a ghetto, but what we call a neighborhood; they haven't got much book learning, but they are not stupid. They don't have good jobs, but they do work hard. They are cheated by neighborhood merchants, black or white. They are abused and brutalized by policemen, black or white. They live near prostitution, narcotics, gambling, and petty crime from which they receive only marginal benefits, and of which they are the greatest victims.

If they are Southerners, they may send their children to integrated schools; that is, schools where the black man who was principal last year is assistant to the assistant principal this year, and where the school song is "Dixie."

Some may be on welfare, which means they barely stay alive while Uncle Sam pays farmers not to farm, tells millionaires they don't have to pay some of their taxes, and Congress barely defeats the new ADA program, the one referring to Aid to Dependent Airlines. They may have a new governor or a new mayor, white, and they may now be discovering that inaugural-day rhetoric is merely a cover for a more sophisticated brand of racist populism. Finally, and increasingly important to us as black politicians holding elective office, our constituents probably vote Democratic as if their lives depended on it.

That last is particularly important because in 1972 we choose a President in this country, and these black voters will be called upon to have at least something to say about who that will be.

Black voters are in the same position with the Democratic Party as the man who was told only two airlines could take him where he wanted to go. One of the two had by far the best safety record but the worst record for hiring black people. He had to decide whether he wanted to be a race man or a live man. That is why independence is important for us. It is not going to be possible for 11 per cent of the population, disorganized and scattered, to form a third party in 1972. It is possible, however, to hold ourselves aloof and independent from some of the hustle and bustle surrounding the myriad Democratic candidates in 1972, even from the one candidate who wins the Democratic Presidential nomination, and then to extract important promises from that Democratic nominee. Or to run our own candidate, a black candidate, for President in states where such a candidacy could affect the outcome.

This is important for black people. Many of us remember the foolish cries of 1968 that urged the election of Richard Nixon on the grounds that his victory would heighten the contradictions, make things worse, hasten the revolution. This is the same kind of sidewalk masochism that elected Adolf Hitler in Germany. It usually comes from people who want our contradictions heightened, not their own.

The plain facts are that heightened political activity on our part is a must in 1972 and beyond. We must beware of those people who urge us to support this or that candidate and instead act strictly in our own interests.

This means defeating not just Richard Nixon, an important task but perhaps an easier job than it might appear when you consider there have been times when the Gallup Poll reported that less than 30 per cent of the population gave Nixon a "good to excellent" rating on the job he is doing. No incumbent President in this century has, since national polls became part of our political life, had such a consistently low rating of approval. The task is not just defeating Nixon but putting into public office all over the country men and women who genuinely care, who care about the problems of the poor and the black and the deprived.

And no one has to recite a long list of these problems. Everyone in the country who has been their victim knows what ravages racism and domestic colonialism have inflicted. The answer to these problems lies with government, no matter what kind of system you live under, and the response to governmental inactivity and indifference is massive agitation and organization.

The mass of American people care little about whether the disadvantaged rise or fall, live or die, and therefore the burden of escape falls on the victims of the crime.

Black people must begin now, in this 1972 election year and afterward, in this country's districts, towns, and cities, the tremendous task of welding together a strong black electorate that will be prepared to make independent decisions about who and what black people vote for and against in the months and years ahead.

There will be those, white and black, who will accuse us and abuse us. These are the pseudomilitants who believe that natural hair can camouflage a processed mind. These are the boutique radicals who would rather debate than do. These are the limousine liberals who must have their manhood insulted before they will give a dollar to help feed the hungry. These are the upright citizens who will tell you that politics is hopeless, corrupt and hopeless, but who give politicians hell when we don't deliver the moon and stars. These are the openhearted people-lovers who want us to sign a petition against discrimination in Ireland but who don't worry about discrimination in their own offices and factories.

These are the people who believe that love will conquer all or that we can smoke America to her knees. If, as in the movie, love means never having to say you're sorry, an awful lot of sorry people have loved making us live sorry lives for 350 years. And, if smoking pot alone would do it, there must be an awful lot of problem-free young people in America today.

Black Americans are from 20 to 70 per cent of the voters in 173 of this country's 435 congressional districts. If we follow the philosophy of Congressman William Clay of St. Louis and remember that we have "no permanent friends, no permanent enemies, only permanent interests," then we can begin to build a black-based political movement that can elect and defeat those who help or hinder us.

We blacks are 45 per cent of New Orleans, 58 per cent of Memphis, 42 per cent of Richmond and Birmingham, 44 per cent of Savannah, nearly 50 per cent of Augusta, and 52 per cent of Greenville, Mississippi. We have got to develop an interest in what happens in these places and in hundreds of towns and counties like them. What happens in Memphis or Newark or Alaska or Alabama to any of us is important to all of us.

But there are alarming signs, the omens, the straws in the wind. The following things all occurred on the same day, Thursday, March 25, 1971:

—The House Internal Security Committee voted to retain the concentration-camp features of the Emergency Detention Act;

—The Department of Health, Education, and Welfare announced that while infant mortality rates for whites had fallen, for black young people they went up;

—Senator Ernest Hollings of South Carolina released studies demonstrating that one-third of the children in rural slums and urban ghettos suffer from retardation;

—The Southern Regional Council in Atlanta asserted that the

federal government's rosy figures on school desegregation were untrue.

Taken separately, these are merely small disruptions in anyone's daily life. Taken together, they are symptomatic of a pernicious national disorder that threatens our lives and well-being.

These separate announcements, and there have been assorted similar announcements since these, ought to be part of a continuous signal to us, a signal that what was wrong is still wrong and what needs to be right will never be right until we ourselves determine that it will be.

It is of course important that those of us who call ourselves politicians, who are elected officials, hold uppermost in our minds the fact that someone chose us. Someone chose us because they thought we'd make life easier. Or better in some way. Higher in quality. More meaningful. We try, most of us as best we can, but something more than that is needed.

We are, we black American politicians, for good or evil, for better or worse, only 1,800 in number. We are far from perfect beings, and as a class of people, we are, proportionately just as dishonest, as crooked, and as calculating as American college students and their professors are.

But the sum of the task for all of us is to fight the evil, racism, and violence that suppress us all, and that will scar all Americans.

Racism and violence should be carefully defined. We know that violence does not limit itself to the bomb at night or the brick through the window or the mugger's knife. And we know that crime and criminality are not limited to the kinds of petty thefts, crimes against property, and crimes of passion that flourish in some black communities. Violence and unchecked criminal elements are running rampant through American life.

It is violent and criminal when black children attend school for twelve years but don't get educated; when black young men represent a disproportionate share of the inductees and casualties in Vietnam; when a ghetto merchant charges 150 per cent interest on a television set or a refrigerator, and wonders why his store is the first one destroyed when the holocaust comes; and when many of America's young people, the very generation we were told was "different" from the rest, show more interest in self-gratification than in the very real problems of the really poor, both black and white.

It is racist, moreover, to suggest that Christopher Columbus "discovered" a country that was already here, inhabited by a thriving and civilized population; it was racist to import people against their will and then impose strange alien ways on them, as it is racist generally for one set of people to impose their cultural values on another.

Until you hear that black people are:

—claiming the superiority of James Brown over Beethoven;

—of the pyramids of Egypt over the Empire State Building;

—of Swahili over French and German and Latin;

—of Langston Hughes and Imamu Baraka over Shelley and Keats and Shakespeare;

—of Jack Johnson, Muhammad Ali, and Jackie Robinson over Gene Tunney, Rocky Marciano, and Brooks Robinson, or of Elijah Muhammad over the Pope . . . why, until you hear these things, then don't accuse us of racism.

Of course, these things are all quite possibly true. But black Americans don't insist that everyone else accept that truth, nor do we control the instruments that make yesterday's lie today's fact.

As we get deeper into the 1970's, the rhetoric of the last twenty years of black struggle must be transformed into new and more intense action. We cannot afford twenty more years of preaching that the hour is *late*. The hour is now. We can't afford the luxury of warning that this is the eleventh hour; it has been midnight since before Nixon took office. The old excuses for inaction are no longer mere cop-outs, they are the badges of cowardice.

Young men and women are desperately needed for struggles in welfare offices, in labor halls, in political wards and precincts, in poverty-ridden communities, in courtrooms, and in the streets. They are not going to be needed in some titanic confrontation in a visionary future; they are needed now, today. Unless they act now, there may not be any later.

We cannot afford the kind of inaction that justifies its existence because the "in" actors are "getting ourselves together." We cannot afford the luxury of deciding that this or that method of achieving social change is too conservative or too militant; we cannot afford to have someone suggest that politics or street demonstrations and/or group economic entrepreneurship or any single method is the only method we can employ to secure our freedom. Nor can we afford to mouth the admirable rhetoric of Malcolm X without also adopting his admirable self-discipline.

We cannot afford to emulate some radical groups that insist their analysis is the only one, or that only "true believers" can participate in what surely must be an all-people's movement.

Perhaps we might be reassured by the thought that while the struggle for racial justice and economic equality is racial in root and while its effects on us are largely economic and psychological, it has an ecological base.

A base that is anti-ecological in the sense that it rejects the proposition that picking up picnic litter from campgrounds will ever be a suitable alternative activity for people who ought to be bringing the polluters of our air, water, and land to public justice in concert with the criminal polluters of our lives, but a problem that is ecological in the very real sense that the men who manufacture garbage to dump in our rivers also manufacture bombs and napalm to dump in the human sea of Vietnam; in the sense that the same people who manufacture automobiles that are no good when they are eighteen months old are the same men who refuse to use their expertise ard skill and capital to manufacture full employment for men.

It is ecological in the sense once stated by Norman Cousins, former editor of the *Saturday Review,* who said:

With all his gifts, man has been able to effect vast change, making his life different from that of those who have lived before. His capacity for invention and his sense of creative splendor have constructed great civilizations. But he has never been in command of his own work. He has never been in balance. The result is that today, for all of his brilliance, he has thrown himself all the way back to his primitive condition, in which his dominant problem on earth was coping with his environment.

To black Americans, this must suggest either accommodating ourselves to the circumstances in which we find ourselves or bending those circumstances to suit our needs, rather than being crushed to suit the needs and entertainment of others.

This requires the realization that there has never been, and never will be, any real Negro problem in America, but that there has been, internationally, the kind of problem spelled out by Dr. Du Bois: "The problem of the 20th century is the problem of the color line, the relation of the darker to the lighter races of men in Asia and Africa and the islands of the sea."

It is this problem that is at the root of every other one. Until it is conquered, we shall all of us suffer together.

XV-
The Need for NAPPI

I<small>F</small> *all* American black people belonged to one organization, one with something like the structure (if not all of the politics) of the NAACP, with a dues-paying membership, with chapters in every state, city, and hamlet, with a paid professional staff to handle problems of health, education, welfare, politics, housing, and the millions of other symptoms of our present dilemma, black Americans would be in much better shape than we are at present.

We could call upon the buying power of our twenty-two million to stop General Motors. We could cast our "balance of power" votes to elect and defeat Presidents and dogcatchers. We could effectively defend our communities from outside or inside attack and subversion.

However, we are not that together. Yet we are an organized people. We belong—depending on our level in society—to a variety of groups.

The last several years have seen a spate of new groupings among all levels of black people. We have seen the rise of Afro-American and black student unions on the college campus; we have seen black caucuses in labor unions, in teachers' groups, on police forces, in religious bodies, and so on. Welfare recipients have formed their own organizations. And black people have always belonged to a variety of social and civic clubs like the East Side Voters League or the Sassy Ladies Savings and Social Club. The Democratic Party has tried to organize black Democratic office-holders; others of us for some reason have remained loyal to the party that we believe freed the slaves.

So we are in many ways a well-organized people. It has occurred to me, however, that there is reason at least to discuss the organization of yet another organization, a network of people primarily interested, though not exclusively, in elective politics as a problem-solving device for black people.

I have concluded that elective politics and the radical, revolutionary change needed in American society are virtually incompatible; however, politics can offer some victories, and ought never be ignored by black people as one weapon in a presently rather empty arsenal.

The passage of the 1965 Voting Rights Act inspired a great deal of hope among Southern black people. That hope has of course not been realized. The elections of Richard Hatcher in Gary, Carl Stokes in Cleveland, Kenneth Gibson in Newark, and the primary victory of Tom Bradley in Los Angeles raised Northern hopes as well. Bradley's defeat and victories for the right, like that in Philadelphia in late 1971, have demonstrated how fragile that hope was. More than seven hundred blacks have been elected to public office in the South. But if public offices were distributed on a representative racial formula, that figure would be more like two thousand.

Once in office, black people, North and South, like Hatcher and Stokes and Gibson as mayors of Northern cities, or the fifteen black state legislators in Georgia, or someone like Mrs. Geneva Collins, Chancery Clerk in Port Gibson, Mississippi, often find their best efforts frustrated by the minority position of black people or the complicated nature of the job at hand.

I suggest the need, then, for an organization that might ease the pre- and post-elective political position of black people in the United States.

First, let us look at existing organizations touching on this field. The two major political parties, through their "minority" offices, will offer minor aid to successful primary candidates of their respective parties. Other sorts of help are offered, for example, by the Voter Education Project, Inc., based in Atlanta, a privately funded voter education and registration project operating in thirteen Deep South states. VEP is handicapped because it must be nonpartisan, and faces a continuing threat of action by Congress to curtail the foundation support VEP has enjoyed in the past. VEP has begun a series of satellite centers established at Southern black schools to aid elected officials.

The Scholarship, Education and Defense Fund for Racial Equality in New York City is an offshoot of the early 60's CORE. It has done some good work in training for voter drives and giving expertise to elected blacks with "special" jobs, e.g., school board members. The Southern Elections Fund represents a relatively new effort to help channel badly needed funds to Democratic, Republican, and independent black candidates in the South, and eventually across the country. This group hopes to fill a void that neither VEP or SEDFRE fill because of their tax-exempt status. One might also list SCLC, NAACP, CORE, ADA, the National Committee for an Effective Congress, and the labor movement, generally, as groups that can be or have been greatly or marginally helpful to black political efforts.

None of these organizations, however, meet a crucial need at present, which is to elect good black candidates and to keep them re-electable by giving them the tools to effect change in their constituencies.

A Richard Hatcher, for instance, may need help in securing federal monies for poverty programs in his city. Where can he turn for help? A Charles Evers needs an "industry hunter" for Fayette, Mississippi. Where can he turn for help? Georgia's black state legislators, provided with no clerical help or office space by the state, need administrative assistants, offices, secretaries. Where can they turn for help? Or suppose John Roosevelt Williams in

Cairo, Illinois, decided he wants to be mayor there. Where does he turn for information on campaign costs, on registration drives, for research on the issues vital to Cairo?

In each of these cases, you turn to your friends. If you are Charles Evers, you can call upon staff members from the Robert Kennedy campaign to help run your campaign. If you are a big-city black mayor, a Jim Gibson from the Potomac Institute will give you some needed technical assistance. If you are Georgia's black legislators, you look to VEP and Clark College's Center for Black Elected Officials for aid and assistance.

Two kinds of aid are needed in two kinds of ways.

Political hopefuls need to know how to get elected and they need it long before election day. After the election is over and they have won, they need information on how to stay elected if they merit it. They need to know how to do the job for which the public has chosen them. They need information on taxes, on municipal bonds, on issues as simple as garbage collection and as complex as the Nigerian conflict. They need a continual supply of technical and political information that is not now readily available from any one source.

There have been attempts to do this last. California State Senator Mervyn Dymally, Illinois State Senator Richard Newhouse, Manhattan Borough President Percy Sutton, Representative John Conyers (D., Michigan), and several others have attempted to organize black elected officials on a national level. Congressman Conyers and others, through the National Committee of Inquiry, have attempted to make the black vote in America a strong political force. Jack Greenberg and the NAACP Legal Defense and Educational Fund have offered research aid for Southern black legislators. Illinois State Senator Newhouse has organized the very effective Black Legislative Clearing House. The Congressional Black Caucus offers some hope of becoming a Washington-centered information group and strong lobby for all black people.

But again, the needed work has not been done.

It can be done, either by strengthening (and perhaps radically altering) the groups mentioned at the beginning of this chapter or by developing new groups and new relationships, putting together new structures to do a new job.

Existing organizations often do not do the job because of statutory restrictions that are a part of their funding. Any frankly political partisan effort must raise the question of fund sources.

I would propose the establishment of a new group that for present purposes might be called "Negroes and Practical Politics, Incorporated." NAPPI* will serve to:

1. Put black political hopefuls in touch with existing organizations.

2. Channel technical pre-election assistance into black campaigns.

3. Put technical expertise in a variety of fields into the hands of black officials.

NAPPI could do this by: (1) locating and identifying those persons with political expertise and with practical, technical knowledge in a variety of government-related fields and (2) establishing contact with black community leaders across the land in an attempt to be on top of developing campaigns. This might be done through a variety of ways: through the present elected officials, through church groups, through NAACP contacts, through the black press, through professional and other associations.

NAPPI would then put persons in the first category in functioning contact with persons in the second category.

For example, the Leadership Conference on Civil Rights has published a bulletin on a regular basis that details what race- or poverty-connected legislation is at what stage in Washington. This kind of information is vital to a black congressional or mayoral candidate, as well as to the black community as a whole.

---

* It may be argued that two groups could better serve this function. Perhaps so, but for discussion's sake, one group will be considered here.

For example, the Center for the Study of Southern Public Policy at Clark College in Atlanta has experimented with a system of "rating" Georgia legislators, using an ADA-like system. This information is vital to potential legislative candidates in the state, and the idea ought to be duplicated in other locations where black candidates are likely to run.

For example, the National Committee for an Effective Congress gives campaign funds to "liberal" House and Senate candidates. It and other groups like it ought to be put in touch with more black hopefuls.

For example, VEP funds voter registration campaigns in Southern communities. VEP and these communities must be aware of one another.

For example, the National League of Cities articulates pro-urban positions that are on occasion vital to black interests. NAPPI could get a candidate for mayor in touch with this organization.

For example, there are on university campuses, in labor, and in business, individuals with great expertise in campaigning. NAPPI should put such persons in touch with hopefuls and should help arrange financing where that is needed. In addition, NAPPI could seek out persons skilled in advertising and the other tools of successful campaigning.

Then NAPPI could work to put the successful candidate, after he or she has won an election, in touch with persons, institutions, and organizations that can play a helpful role. NAPPI might be able to put a Charles Evers in touch with businessmen interested in helping poor black people and thus help provide the technical expertise necessary for Fayette, Mississippi, to lure an industry. NAPPI might help the Fayette City Council float bonds, secure underwriting, and could insure that whatever industry comes would not be exploitative.

Continuing in this vein, surely NAPPI could have helped Mayor Evers make a better choice of training site for his policemen than Mayor Rizzo's Philadelphia. And, for example, NAPPI could act as go-between for black state legislators and city councilmen and the Law Students Civil Rights Research Council and the Black Law Students Association to recruit, train, and fund law students to work with elected officials as aides.

NAPPI could put any of the authors of the immense number of scholarly papers and surveys on a variety of urban and state governmental concerns in contact with the black public officials in positions to put theory into practice.

As final example, NAPPI could insure that no black elected official, whether he is a police juror in West Feliciana Parish, Louisiana, or chairman of a subcommittee of the U.S. House of Representatives, goes without the information and resources he needs to do his job.

If some of these things sound simple or routine or easy, then let me stress that they are not, simply because most black candidates for office, at whatever level, do not have the advantage of these contacts and possibilities.

In the late 1960's, I spent some months on a project for the Southern Regional Council, interviewing many of the black candidates who had sought office in the South in the wake of discovering that, at last, black people in their areas could vote. It is remarkable how difficult a task campaigning is for a people unused to, and often used by, politics.

XVI-
America's Revolution

> *. . . people and governments never have learned*
> *anything from history . . .*
> —GEORG WILHELM FRIEDRICH HEGEL, 1832

A PART OF the politics of the streets is moving indoors In the 1970's we must translate the politics of marches and demonstrations and protests into an effective electoral instrument. This special kind of merger of street politics and electoral politics characterized many of the public events of the 1960's and the early maneuvering for the 1972 Presidential election. But the merger is not yet complete.

The necessary new politics of the 1970's can take form only if the lessons and struggles of the past two decades, especially of the 1960's, become genuine building blocks for the future. The danger is that those lessons may be pushed aside and forgotten even by some of the people who took part in that learning process. Hegel was right in suggesting that people and governments seem often to learn nothing from their past, even the immediate past.

The history of black activity in America in the 1960's frequently involved street politics to force legislative action to benefit black

154

people. The sit-ins of the early 60's made possible the public-accommodations provisions of the 1964 Civil Rights Act. The freedom rides gave backbone to the Interstate Commerce Commission and made it enforce existing regulations barring segregation in interstate travel and encouraged the commission to promote new regulations covering intrastate travel. Early activities by the Student Nonviolent Coordinating Committee in Mississippi in the early 1960's, and in Selma, Alabama, in 1963, aided later by Dr. King and the Southern Christian Leadership Conference, culminated in the Selma-Montgomery March. That confrontation led finally to the 1965 Voting Rights Act, and to President Lyndon Johnson's televised promise that "we shall overcome."

Johnson's political reputation sank with the disasters of his Vietnam policy. Perhaps it is, however, worth remembering that there was no more eloquent voice in America in March of 1965 when Johnson delivered that voting rights speech. It has been described as the most emotional speech of his career.

At times, history and fate meet at a single time in a single place to shape a turning point in man's unending search for freedom.

So it was at Lexington and Concord. So it was a century ago at Appomattox. So it was last week in Selma, Alabama. . . .

There is no Negro problem. There is no Southern problem. There is no Northern problem. There is only an American problem. . . .

There is no constitutional issue here. The command of the Constitution is plain. There is no moral issue. It is wrong—deadly wrong—to deny any of your fellow Americans the right to vote in this country.

There is no issue of states' rights or national rights. There is only the struggle for human rights. . . .*

* Lyndon B. Johnson, speech before joint session of U.S. Congress, March 15, 1965.

Johnson's determination and the mood of the country were right for passing the 1965 Voting Rights Act. Yet his conclusion, though still eloquent, was not entirely accurate in what was to follow.

What happened in Selma is part of a far larger movement which reaches into every section and state of America. It is the effort of American Negroes to secure for themselves the full blessings of American life.

Their cause must be our cause too. Because it is not just Negroes, but really it is all of us who must overcome the crippling legacy of bigotry and injustice. And we shall overcome. . . .

. . . This great rich, restless country can offer opportunity and education and hope to all—all, black and white, all, North and South, sharecropper and city dweller.

These are the enemies: poverty, ignorance, disease. They are our enemies, not our fellow man, not our neighbor. And these enemies too—poverty, disease, and ignorance—we shall overcome. . . .*

The words were fine, particularly fine for a Southern President. But the realities of the late 1960's and early 1970's were not the battles against poverty and disease but the battles that destroyed villages in Vietnam, and civilians on the ground maimed and killed by our bombs, comfortably so since our pilots didn't even have to see the blood and the shattered limbs. The fact of hungry children in this country, children who literally do not get enough to eat, is now undisputed by many. But we still live with a government capable, as the Nixon Administration showed in late 1971, of attempting to cut down the lists of those who benefit from food-stamp programs so that it can hold the U.S. Department of Agriculture budget lower even than the amount appropriated by Congress.

The battles fought and won by black people in the 60's led

* *Ibid.*

largely to surface gains. The public-accommodations legislation and the regulations on interstate travel benefited mostly the emerging black middle class. The black underclass has benefited only marginally, even from the Voting Rights Act.

To repeat the methods of the 1960's in this new decade and attain similar, or greater, gains for any class of black people—or for the poor, white or black—will be difficult.

For one thing, the sympathy in the North that was aroused by police dogs in Greenwood, Mississippi, and fire hoses in Birmingham has been replaced by a growing conservatism as the Southern "black problem" has moved North. Additionally, the very real human problems of poverty and social pathology resulting from institutional racism are not soluble by the stroke of the same pen that eliminated one of the two separate lunch counters in every Southern department store or the "Colored" and "White" signs from thousands of Southern bathrooms or the impossible features of Southern literacy tests.

The strategy that made it possible for black voters to register in Fayette, Mississippi, so they could elect Charles Evers their mayor will not adapt itself easily toward providing Fayette's citizens—or the citizens of any other hamlet or city—with jobs and houses and incomes and education. New strategies must be devised, new techniques developed, and new goals outlined.

The standard 1960's liberal agenda of adequate housing for all, full employment, and an end to overseas imperialism can be achieved only through a more sophisticated approach that will mesh street politics with increasingly complicated legislative goals. This desire, this aim, is reflected in part in the attempts—unsure and uneven—of black politicians to set a national agenda for the 1972 Presidential election.

This desire is seen too in the growing awareness among all nonwhite Americans who struggle with the techniques popularized by blacks in the 1960's and who then often move into a radical kind of electoral politics. It was exemplified in early 1972 when

George Wiley, director of the National Welfare Rights Organization, called for each of his thousands of members to become active in local delegate races for the Democratic national convention. It is also evident in the growing politicizing of the issue groups, largely white and middle class, who are concerned about peace, consumerism, women's rights, and the environment.

Following an example set in an earlier period of racial turmoil by the abolitionists, and in another period of moral turmoil by the prohibitionists, these issue groups are turning toward a new kind of politics, largely aimed at victory within the Democratic Party but with an independence born of struggle against county courthouse gangs and city hall bosses on another battlefield, the streets. The nonwhite ethnic groups want control, for jobs and the other bread-and-butter rewards of politics; the issue groups want a shift in the national consciousness that will translate itself into legislative approval of their goals.

Together, they stand against the old New Deal coalition, made up of the white South, organized labor, and the big-city machines. Their challenge for the 1970's—the challenge of the nonwhite ethnics and the issue groups—is whether they can stand together on issues of common concern long enough to overcome old coalitions.

Part of the answer lies in changes in the political processes of this nation. John F. Kennedy once compared political relationships to a galaxy with stars and planets and moons all pulling at one another with varying degrees of force. His point was that to shift one section of that firmament, one planet or star, was to affect and change all the rest of it. Something akin to that kind of shifting and changing *has* occurred, particularly within the Democratic Party, in terms of the procedures of national conventions.

Most of this country's political processes have evolved, often in ways that would have quite amazed the founding fathers. Initially, it was not even clear exactly how the Electoral College was supposed finally to vote for the President of the United States.

Thomas Jefferson was elected only after a challenge from Aaron Burr. Burr was assumed to be the Vice-Presidential candidate, but both Presidential and Vice-Presidential candidates were voted on by the electors of the Electoral College. Since Burr had as many votes as Jefferson, he claimed the Presidency.

National political conventions, as we know them, are a relatively modern invention. By the 1960's, the national conventions of both the Republican and the Democratic national political parties had become completely dominated by party regulars. Those party regulars held absolute sway in nominating candidates for President and Vice-President. Alabama Governor George Wallace, with only 13.5 per cent of the vote in 1968, was yet the most successful third-party Presidential candidate in the nation in almost fifty years. In effect, then, this has meant that one of the men chosen at the two major national conventions was almost inevitably going to be President of the United States.

As one political analysis had it, the paramount function of the conventions, the selection of the Presidential and Vice-Presidential nominees, "lends great importance to the selection of delegates to the national convention. In view of this vital function, it might be supposed that there would be widespread popular interest and vigilance in the selection of delegates. Yet it is estimated that 97 per cent of the voters have no participation in the selection of two-thirds of the delegates who are sent to national conventions to nominate presidential candidates."*

This was true through the 1968 conventions. Senator Eugene McCarthy "took it to the country," as he put it, in challenging the incumbent President of his own party in Presidential primaries on the issue of Vietnam. His showing in the New Hampshire primary and the evident dissatisfaction in the nation probably forced President Johnson from office. But it had limited effect on the

---

* "U.S. Politics, Inside and Out," *U.S. News & World Report,* published by Macmillan, New York, 1970.

convention nominating process. The late Senator Robert Kennedy was perhaps the one man who could have challenged that process and carried the day at the Chicago convention. The convention itself chose to hand the nomination to a party regular, Vice-President Hubert Humphrey.

In truth, the idea that Presidential primaries ever gave the people a chance to nominate a Presidential candidate is largely a myth. John Kennedy put together a string of primary victories in 1960, but he had also got commitments from a substantial number of influential political figures and delegates in states with no primaries.

At the Republican national convention in 1968, only 509 of 1,333 delegates came from primary states. At the Democratic convention, 1,106 votes were from primary state delegates, compared to 1,516 delegates from nonprimary states. Delegates from nonprimary states wielded an absolute majority of the votes in both conventions.

I took part in a challenge to this system in 1968. It was only partially successful, but it did help create the necessary impetus for Democratic Party reforms. I was cochairman of the Georgia challenge delegation that attacked the hand-picked slate of Governor Lester Maddox. The Georgia delegation was as closed-shop an operation as can be imagined. The Democratic state executive committee picked the delegates and, as a practical matter, this meant usually selecting friends of the incumbent governor, either his friends or people he could control.

In 1968, the national convention voted finally to seat only half the challenge delegation, but the process of reform had begun. Under this pressure, the national Democratic Party has begun to make it possible for people to have some voice in and to participate in the process of selecting the delegates who nominate the candidate. Early delegate elections in 1972 in some states produced surprises. And the process of change has only begun. The old convention system will never be the same again.

The question that remains, however, is, can a new political

coalition happen in the 1970's? Can the people so long cut off from real political influence form a winning national coalition? It is only possible if those who became politically aware in the 1960's can now adapt to the opportunities of the 1970's. One young activist has written:

Every man has his own sense of crisis and outrage. So long as this is not shared or widely shared, most of us deal with it, suffer from it, repress and forget it, in private. The solitary prophet makes his own wilderness of inattention, mockery, and withdrawal by talking to people unwilling to listen. It is (sometimes) worth trying, but most of us learn to keep quiet. Political action is only possible when expressions of outrage and prophecies of disaster meet a lively response, at least within some circle of our own acquaintances. We try them out on our friends. The actual decision to enter the political arena will almost certainly be made by a small group, but it should only be made by a group whose members have what might be called intimations of growth. Where do such intimations come from? Hopefully, from conversations and encounters with other people, hints of commitment, plausible signs of interest. Would-be activists must have some sense of their future constituency; they must know that so many people will support the strike, attend the mass meeting, join the march, before they put themselves forward and call for action.*

The opportunity for new coalitions in American politics exists today, in 1972 and beyond, as it never has before. It is not just that street politics has moved toward at least partial political participation in the elective processes, it is also that there is a real potential for involving enormous numbers of people in the political business who are now not even involved in voting. One of every three eligible citizens failed to vote in the 1964 Presidential election. Fully 39 per cent of the eligible voters failed to vote in 1968.

* Michael Walzer, *Political Action*. Quadrangle Books, Chicago, 1971.

A Gallup study of nonvoters in 1968 placed the majority of them in two categories: fifteen million voters registered but without interest enough to vote and ten million who could have registered but did not. Surely among these twenty-five million nonvoters there are many who simply feel cut out of participation in the processes of government.

It is my belief that nonwhite Americans and other issue-oriented Americans can come together in a political coalition over such concerns as Vietnam and America's role in the world, on racial justice, on consumerism, on women's rights, and on concern for the environment.

Booker T. Washington is often quoted as a great black American leader of the late nineteenth century. He was that, though his famous speech in 1895 on black and white relationships, which came to be called the "Atlanta Compromise" speech, had enough of the sound of segregation in it to be quite acceptable to many white segregationists.

A young black college teacher, John Hope, was among those listening to Washington's speech. He thought long about it and gave his own more militant views in a speech a year later. They could apply today to nonwhite Americans.

If we are not striving for equality, in heaven's name for what are we living? . . . If money, education, and honesty will not bring to me as much privilege, as much equality as they bring to any American citizen, then they are to me a curse, and not a blessing. God forbid that we should get the implements with which to fashion our freedom, and then be too lazy or pusillanimous to fashion it. Let us not fool ourselves or be fooled by others. If we cannot do what other freemen do, then we are not free. . . . In this Republic we shall be less than freemen, if we have whit less than that which thrift, education, and honor afford other freemen. . . . Rise, Brothers! . . . Be as restless as the tempestuous billows on the boundless sea. Let your discontent break mountain-high against the wall of prejudice, and swamp it to the very foundation. Then we shall not have to plead for justice nor on bended knee crave mercy; for we shall be men. Then and not until then will liberty in its highest sense be the boast of our Republic.*

ABOUT THE AUTHOR

JULIAN BOND was born in 1940 in Nashville, Tennessee, and is a graduate of Morehouse College in Atlanta. He was a founder of the Student Nonviolent Coordinating Committee, of which he was Communications Director from 1960–1965. Since 1965, Mr. Bond has been an elected member of the Georgia House of Representatives. Refused admission because of anti-war activities, Mr. Bond has served in that body only since 1967, after the U.S. Supreme Court ordered him seated. At the 1968 Democratic convention in Chicago, he led a challenge delegation to the hand-picked Georgia slate of Governor Lester Maddox.

Mr. Bond lives in Atlanta with his wife and five children.